Law and Psychology

Law and Psychology

Papers Presented at
SSRC Law and Psychology
Conferences 1979–1980

Edited by
Sally Lloyd-Bostock

SSRC Centre for Socio-legal Studies
Wolfson College
Oxford

Published in 1981 by the
SSRC Centre for Socio-legal Studies
Wolfson College
Oxford

ISBN 0–86226–075–2

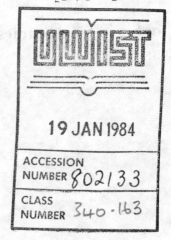

Contents

Preface

The papers in this collection were originally presented at two meetings of the SSRC Law and Psychology Seminar Group, held in Oxford during 1979–1980. This was the third year that the Centre for Socio–Legal Studies, Oxford, had held regular Law and Psychology conferences. The conferences provide an opportunity (which is still very rare in this country), for lawyers and psychologists to become acquainted with each other, and to hear about and discuss psychology and law research and its applications. Practising as well as academic lawyers and psychologists have attended the conferences and their response has been highly enthusiastic and encouraging.

Earlier meetings in the series introduced the longer-established topics in the law and psychology field such as the reliability of testimony. The aim of the 1979–1980 meetings was partly to examine in more depth some issues which had given rise to vigorous discussion at previous meetings, such as the roles of psychologists as experts, and the problems in reconciling legal and psychological models of man. The meetings aimed also to provide an opportunity for new or unusual areas of work, which might be at an early stage of development, to be discussed. A natural consequence of this is diversity in the topics of the papers, which include pre-trial publicity, the psychological impact of being the victim of a crime, research at Broadmoor Hospital, and aspects of subjective probability. The collection comprises mainly papers from the September 1979 meeting. However, there was a strong international representation at the smaller, March 1980 meeting, and two papers presented by overseas speakers at that meeting have been included – those by Neil Vidmar from Canada and Günter Bierbrauer from Germany – Both in the general area of legal dispute resolution.

The Law and Psychology Seminar Group is funded by the SSRC, and the meetings are held under the auspices of the Centre for Socio-Legal Studies in Oxford, which provides the considerable administrative and secretarial support needed. In addition to acknowledging this support I would particularly like to thank John Boal for his help in editing the papers and arranging for their publication.

December 1980

SALLY LLOYD-BOSTOCK
(Convenor of the SSRC
Law and Psychology
Seminar Group)

Preface

SALLY LLOYD-BOSTOCK

Educational Psychologists and the Juvenile Court

GEOFF MOSS* AND ANDREW SUTTON†

Introduction

Psychology as a provider of expert witness to the courts may yet be at an early stage of its development in this country. But there is one particular branch of psychology already well established in the routine provision of expertise on a proportionately large scale. In a recent national survey of the educational psychologists[1] employed by local education authorities (Wedell and Lambourne, 1979) 45 per cent of the respondents stated that they averaged at least once-monthly contacts with child and adolescent offenders, while 20 per cent estimated that at least once a month they worked in the Observation and Assessment Centres of social services departments.

At the time of that survey there were about 900 educational psychologists in post in local authorities in England and Wales. Assuming that by now the figure is nearer 1000 we can estimate approximately 200 psychologists in England and Wales who at least once a month go into Observation and Assessment Centres for the purposes of providing psychological assessments of children many of whom will pass before the juvenile court. We can also assume that around 450 psychologists in all have at least once-monthly contacts with known juvenile delinquents in a variety of contexts. Assuming that the responses to the survey fairly represented the facts (Sutton, 1978), then educational psychologists probably provide the bulk of psychological evidence presented to English courts. Given the quantity of their work for the courts, then the quality of that work, we suggest, merits some concern.

Because educational psychologists are employed within local government service there exists no central source of information about their activities. This

---

*Senior Educational psychologist, Child and Family Guidance Service, Avon.

†Centre for Child Study, Faculty of Education, University of Birmingham.

paper seeks to assemble an overall impression of the educational psychologist in the juvenile court, drawn from the fragments of published material on the subject and small-scale enquiries undertaken by ourselves.

Development of Educational Psychology

Educational psychology has frequently traced its origins back to the early work of Sir Cyril Burt for the London County Council where he worked part-time from 1913 to 1932. The limited expansion of educational psychology before and after World War II, however, depended largely upon the spread of the child guidance movement, which provided the psychologist with a role which was largely clinical rather than directed towards scientific research. The major link between Burt's work and that of his successors was their mutual (though differing) emphasis on the use of psychometric tests. Educational psychologists remained a rare resource, and even at the beginning of this decade there were still a few local authorities which did not employ even one. Rapid expansion in training in the early 1970s combined with local authority reorganization to create the present pattern of professional employment, in which every local education authority now provides a 'psychological service' comprising a hierarchy of senior and junior posts.

Educational psychology is a relatively venerable and substantial branch of applied psychology in this country. If one does indeed trace its origins back to Burt then it had an early concern in the evaluation and treatment of delinquent children. In *The Young Delinquent* he advocated a scientific approach which, whatever criticisms may be levelled at other aspects of this book or at his later work, may still stand as a model for thorough psychological investigation.

First, a systematic survey of the whole situation as it is at present. Secondly, a genetic (i.e. historical) study of the history of the offender throughout his past, and thirdly, a trial scheme of recommendations regarding treatment in the future, all checked and supplemented as time goes on, by an after-study of the effects secured. (Burt, 1925, p. 11).

If the origins of educational psychology are traced back to the child guidance movement then the same early concern with delinquency emerges, since a prime intention of that movement was to 'prevent' later adult crime and disturbance by early intervention in the psychodynamics then considered causative of such later behaviours.

For a long time educational psychologists had little contact with the juvenile court, being fully occupied with the demands generated within the local education authorities themselves (see Summerfield, 1968). In the 1960s three local authority children's departments, feeling the need for psychological involvement in the juvenile court system and being unable to obtain this from their overtaxed local education authority psychology services, created their own specialist autonomous services, in two cases in collaboration with their public health departments. These three services, Torbay, Exeter and Birmingham, were closely involved with the juvenile courts. Both clinical and educational psychologists were employed in these services which disappeared in various reorganizations in the early 1970s. The enlarged local education authority psychology services only took up and routinized juvenile court work in the mid-1970s. By the end of the 1970s provision of some sort of psychological service to the juvenile courts by local education authority educational psychologists seemed established as a regular practice in most, perhaps all, local authorities – the provision being made through the court services organized by social services departments.

It should be noted that in local education authorities generally the provision of psychologists is a discretionary power, and none of the functions that they fulfill are statutorily defined or imposed. The widespread role that they have recently adopted with regard to the juvenile justice system is similarly discretionary. Nowhere are educational psychologists mentioned in a statute or statutory instrument at the present time in English law[2].

Training of Educational Psychologists

Although there is no 'official' requirement for a local authority educational psychologist to possess certain qualifications (unlike the NHS requirement for clinical psychologists) – so that a local authority could appoint anybody, regardless of qualifications, as an 'educational psychologist' – in practice there is a fairly well agreed standard of training required. According to both the British Psychological Society and the Association of Educational Psychologists the appropriate training for an educational psychologist is:
1 an honours degree in psychology (or appropriate equivalent graduate qualification recognised by the BPS);
2 a minimum of 2 years teaching experience; and
3 a recognized award (formerly Diploma, now Masterate in Educational Psychology) following completion of a 1-year course of postgraduate training.

The content of these 1-year professional training courses varies considerably, some with emphasis still upon the traditional psychometric approach, at least one course favouring a largely psychoanalytic orientation, and at least one other stressing a systems-theory application. The historical basis for most training was indeed in mental measurement, in particular the normative measurement of intelligence and educational achievement. Of late, though, there has been a movement within the profession, reflected in changes in the curriculum emphasis of the training courses, towards a proactive rather than reactive style of working. Gillham (1978) has presented a series of alternative approaches to the conventional model.

But although psychologists claim to want new ways of working, examination of the literature written by educational psychologists about what they do finds little evidence of tried or evaluated practice. From such a survey of the literature Hart and Taylor (1979) have recently concluded that while many modern educational psychologists may discredit the 'tester' role, it is still the most often written about, and while they may espouse more radical ways of working there is scant literature about such projects' actually being put into practice.

As educational psychologists are employed by education departments, it has long been established that a prerequisite experience should be a minimum of 2 years' classroom teaching. This requirement from time to time becomes an issue, with its opponents claiming that it probably has little value for a would-be applied psychologist. It remains the case, however, that such school-teaching experience is still favoured as an essential prerequisite for any psychologist who is going to work in the education service. Yet though it is also the case that educational psychologists will be expected to offer their professional skills to social services departments in roles that include the assessment of young offenders, no analogous previous work experience there is considered necessary. In other words, for many educational psychologists, the first experience that they will have of the legal, administrative and social systems for juvenile delinquents and others before the juvenile court is when they are first required to 'assess' such a child, and write a report to the magistrate about him. So it would not be surprising were educational psychologists to construe that child, his problems and needs, within the particular framework of his training and experience. Perhaps a differently trained and experienced psychologist might approach the task in a different way.

We should be asking, 'What are the appropriate training experiences for such a task? Why an *educational* psychologist?' Apart from the fact that, as a body, they have been established longer and more plentifully than any other psychological practitioners (in many areas of England and Wales they hold the monopoly on child psychology), it could be argued that they are particularly experienced in dealing with *children*. At one level one might respond that a modern understanding of development and behaviour demands that this be qualified as 'children in education', whereas juvenile court work involves the consideration of children in sometimes very different contexts indeed. But there is another aspect to the question. Here we become caught up in the interaction between psychological theory and the socio-legal system. Without a separate court system for children would we require child psychologists to be involved?

Development of the Juvenile Court

The development of both the juvenile court and the system of punishment of young offenders is bound up with the development of the concept of childhood. The present concept contains within it the somewhat vaguely defined notion of immaturity which dates back in this country to early nineteenth-century thinking about juvenile crime. Previously a child could be tried and sentenced as if he were an adult. He might be imprisoned, transported or executed for a crime provided the prosecution case was made that the child knew his conduct was wrong. If detained, the child went to the same prison as an adult.

Early changes of attitudes were shown in an Act of 1838 establishing a separate prison (Parkhurst on the Isle of Wight) for juvenile delinquents, to remove them from the corrupting influence of mature wrong-doers. Subsequent Acts of 1847 (Trial and Punishment of Juvenile Offenders) and 1879 (Summary Jurisdiction Act) took most children out of the High Courts by giving magistrates powers to try them. By the Children's Act 1908, separate courts for children were finally introduced to meet the following requirements:

(i)   that child offenders should be kept separate from adult offenders;

(ii)   that they should not be sent to prison as a punishment or deterrent to crime;

(iii)   that they should receive a different form of treatment because of their special needs;

(iv)   that parents should have some responsibility for their children's behaviour (hence the magistrates could impose fines upon them for the misdemeanours of their children).

The Children and Young Persons Act, 1933, continued this development of separating crime from punishment by establishing the principle that the juvenile court should sentence young offenders according to their *needs* not according to the seriousness of the offence. Note that this was contemporary with the development of the child guidance movement. The offence was now an indication of need, which need, perhaps, social intervention might be able to meet. Behind every act there must be some deeper, hidden motive. Wrongdoing, then, was a symptom of some larger malaise. Care proceedings and criminal proceedings could, under this principle, sit together in the same court system. This philosophy was well described in 1942 by the then senior chairman of the Inner London Juvenile Courts (Watson, 1942, pp. 88–89):

After determining the facts, the magistrate is required to take steps for removing a child or young person from undesirable surroundings. To carry out this instruction the court requires an inquiry into what those surroundings are.

He went on to make the point that the offence itself is not as important as the social conditions of the child:

In my experience, even when the offence appears to be trivial, it is by no means always safe to deal with the offender without looking any further at what he has done. A trifling offence may be symptomatic of conditions which urgently require treatment. If therefore the court has any doubts it is better to resolve them by requiring a report upon the child which may prove superfluous than by omitting to do so which may lead to disaster.

This notion of delinquency in the young as having psychosocial pathology is described later:

I must explain that in London we are fortunate in having medico-psychologists or psychiatrists – the terms are synonymous – attached to the remand homes and reception centres. . . . But they are only able to deal with a fraction of the cases which come before the juvenile courts. Therefore it is the responsibility of the magistrates to decide at the first hearing whether a special examination of this nature is necessary or not. This is far from easy; indeed it would be difficult for an expert, let alone a layman, to detect unerringly during a brief appearance in court every case where a normal exterior serves to conceal some deep-rooted mental condition. The ideal arrangement would be for the courts to receive a medical report upon *every* child appearing before it (except for a technical or trivial offence). This is the practice in some states in America and its adoption in this country is long overdue.

The present practice derives from the Children and Young Persons Act, 1969. Under this act the intention was that the juvenile court should proceed only as a civil court for anyone legally defined as a child, the minimum age of criminal responsibility being changed from 10 years to 14 years, while for young persons (14–17 years) the juvenile court should retain both civil and criminal functions, the latter being restricted. At the same time, the Act also extended the powers and discretion of social services departments. Supervision orders replaced probation for children under 14 years, and Intermediate Treatment was introduced. In the only handbook of educational psychology practice providing guidance for practitioners (*The Practice of Educational Psychology*) Chazan, Moore, Willams and Wright (1974), commenting upon these changes, observe: 'One may expect the educational psychologist even more than in the past to contribute to the preliminary social enquiries made by the local authority and presented in court in a written report . . . sound diagnosis leads to suitable treatments' (p. 53).

Psychological Reports to the Juvenile Court

For juveniles, therefore, there has now arrived the circumstance, long sought by many reformers, in which all children identified by the legal systems are processed primarily by a system of child welfare, and further, in many parts of the country, this processing may involve an 'assessment' or 'diagnosis' by a psychologist as a routinized part of its procedures.

Before describing the main route to such psychological investigations, it is worth accounting some of the byways through which a psychologist's findings may come to the juvenile court. Firstly, there are the informal routes *via* the reports of others. This may even occur quite without the knowledge of the psychologist involved – for example, the mandatory school report may include extracts from some earlier psychological report deposited in the child's personal school records. Such a mention might wholly omit the source of the information given, and reduce it to what the teacher regards as its essence, for example 'IQ 86'. Similarly the home circumstances report of a probation officer or social worker might include information from or about a child's earlier contact with a child guidance centre, and again it is possible that information from a psychologist's report might be selected and quoted without reference to its author. Despite the recent national concern over confidentiality it remains the general reality that professional reports once circulated become common property.

Secondly, there exist a variety of *ad hoc* ways in which a psychologist's evidence might be specially prepared for the juvenile court. A juvenile court might request a psychiatric report, and this might only be conveniently arranged through a child or adolescent facility within the NHS. Often when this occurs the psychiatrist preparing the report will arrange for a clinical psychologist to contribute to the examination. When this occurs the clinical psychologist's findings might be incorporated into the psychiatrist's report: Ward (1978) has raised certain legal questions attendant upon such an arrangement. Alternatively they may be presented directly to the court in the form of a separate, accompanying report. Another *ad hoc* procedure, apparently largely dependent upon local conditions and personal contacts, is for a social worker, knowing that a given child is shortly to appear in court, to ask an educational psychologist to prepare a court report in advance of that appearance. This may involve a child already known to that psychologist, or it may involve a wholly new investigation.

A further occasional source of psychological reports is provided by the Classifying Schools, those five ex-Approved Schools with special assessment facilities and their own psychologists. Particular children may find their way to the juvenile courts *via* such establishments (for example, children who offend whilst absconding). The psychological assessments from such schools tend to be incorporated into an overall assessment document, and presumably present the same sort of legal, technical and ethical problems as when psychologists' findings are buried in psychiatric reports (c.f. Ward, 1978). The psychologists involved may be clinical, educational, or without either such professional qualification (Porteus, 1978).

'Observation and Assessment'

The main road to a psychologist's court report, however, lies for most children through the social services departments' 'observation and assessment centres'. Section 36 (4) (b) of the Children and Young Persons Act, 1969, had stipulated that every regional plan for child care should include proposals . . .

. . . for the provision of facilities for the observation of the physical and mental condition of children in the care of the relevant authorities and for the assessment of the most suitable accommodation and treatment for those children.

Whatever the original intention of those who framed this section, and whatever the range of possible interpretations of how precisely these requirements might be fulfilled, in practice the local authorities have implemented them largely in terms of establishing *centres*, nearly all residential establishments, to which children are admitted to be 'observed and assessed'.

The theoretical justification for such provision owes much implicitly to Burt's *The Young Delinquent*, being expressed most articulately in its modern manifestation by Hoghughi (1979) in the proposition that human behaviour is within certain limits predictable, that an individual may be distinguishable by the relative constancy of certain characteristic behaviours, and that his susceptibility to change is an important aspect of any evaluation of these matters. This position is of course itself open to criticism. Additionally, Hoghughi's own establishment is the only one under the direction of a psychologist, and as he has pointed out there tends to be little or no recognition within the social services system of the enormous technical problems of 'observing' and 'assessing' human behaviour. As psychologists we can only say that the lack of psychological sophistication of those running observation and assessment centres can be truly monumental.

The observation and assessment centres and the services that they provide vary enormously, even within a single authority. Typically such a centre might accommodate around 24 children of both sexes, though there are still single-sex establishments, usually for older children and more difficult cases. The children living there might have been sent by a court on an interim court order 'for reports', or they might have been placed there informally by the social services department for its own purposes. Some of the inmates will be under active assessment, others might have completed this process, remaining at the observation and assessment centre until a suitable placement turns up. Such waits can be considerable. Cooper (1975) found that the difficulty of moving children on was the main bone of contention of the heads of observation and assessment centres in Birmingham. In two of the centres 48 per cent of the children had been with them for more than three months, and one child had been there for more than a year. Many centres include 'schooling' on the premises, with teachers seconded full-time from the local education authority, others send their children out to local schools, and in some cases the child may not have received education at all during his stay. The cases sent by the juvenile court will include the whole range of indictable offences that may be committed by juveniles, as well as the nonindictable issues, such as nonschool attendance, place of safety, moral danger. Recommendations for disposal at the end of assessment are largely directed into the child care system, for example, supervision at home, a care order (including 'home on trial', children's home and 'community home with education') and intermediate treatment.

The mechanisms of this assessment vary vastly. Characteristically, details on the child's background, his home life, etc. will be contributed by the already prepared home circumstances reports and school reports, supplemented in some cases by additional details by a social worker if this is possible, and by the residential staff's impressions of the child's parents on their visits. The residential and teaching staff will contribute direct impressions of the child and in many cases the child will be 'seen' by a visiting psychologist and psychiatrist. Often, through not inevitably, these visitors will contribute to a case conference where the recommendations of the observation and assessment centre are finalized and drafted into a report. Both psychologist and psychiatrist will report separately.

The psychologist will be an educational psychologist working for the local education authority. Typically (s)he will visit the observation and assessment centre regularly on a sessional basis, maybe once, maybe several times a week. Most psychologists will be contributing these sessions as part of a week that is largely given over to school psychological service or child guidance work, and some at least appear to resent this committment of time that drains from what they regard as their central role. In a few instances, however, the psychologist is a 'specialist', which implies a full-time appointment to such work rather than any necessary practical background or research interest. The psychologist will probably see both 'court' and 'noncourt' cases; that is, both children who are on interim orders and children who are there for the private purposes of the social services department. Typically, the psychologist's major output will be in the form of a 'report'. When a court case is involved the overwhelming majority of psychologists involved will not expect to appear personally in court to support their evidence under cross-examination, and, on the basis of practice to date, will indeed never be called.

It would be interesting to document the process of observation and assessment from the point of view of its subjects – the children who pass through it. It is a large population (5300 of the 99,000 children in care in 1975), diverse in many respects but having in common a lack of skills of the sort needed to make their voices heard. We can try to consider the phenomenon of residential observation and assessment from the point of view of our own children, or the child that we all once were, but this is at best a shaky exercise because of the vast differences that separate our own personal experiences from those of the modal observation and assessment client. We may, however, make certain general observations about aspects of residential 'observation and assessment' centres that have a likely bearing upon the children's personal responses. The child has often been taken to the observation and assessment centre, perhaps forcibly, and separated from his parents and familiar neighbourhood maybe for the first time in his life. He is taken to an institution where he is placed in a group of strange children (spanning maybe eight years in age range), some of whom are old hands who have been there a considerable time already, some indeed having spent their whole lives being shifted from one institution to another. The adults in charge are probably 'caring', concerned to produce a 'supportive group situation', keen to 'establish relationships' (for most children rather unfamiliar behaviours in authority figures). But for most practical purposes he is alone to fend for himself, miles from his folks, sleeping in a dormitory, spending his days in a 'schoolroom' with teachers who do not understand how *he* has been taught to do take-aways, with no-one who shares his own personal, private vocabulary, fears and values. Often he will not know precisely why he is there, what precisely he must do to get out, or even whether he will ever get out at all. He may well arrive with an understanding of his three weeks' interim order 'for reports' as being a three-week sentence, after which he will go home. He will likely find others who came several months back with the same understanding, and are still wondering where they are going to go next. Indeed there is a new world view that has to be learned from the other more sophisticated inmates in order to survive within the culture of care, with unfamiliar concepts that include a whole range of perhaps even worse places that he might be sent to. There is also a baffling array of unfamiliar adults with unclear roles, 'care staff', 'your social worker', 'the doctor', and just plain Mr or Mrs – . These people are generally friendly (perhaps in stark contrast to others that he has met in his progress through the judicial process), and for adults, most uncharacteristically keen to talk about the most extraordinary topics, often wholly unrelated to anything that the child (or his family) might understand to be linked with his present predicament.

It is here, as he struggles to find and adopt an appropriate façade to this strange and uncertain world with its odd adults wielding apparently total and arbitrary authority over his destiny, as he fights (in some cases physically) to find his niche in the inmate subculture of his peer group, with no clear idea of what his future might be or what precisely he must do or how he must behave to secure it, that he is 'observed and assessed', and meets the psychologist.

The Educational Psychologist's Contribution

The Literature

What does the psychologist do when (s)he meets the child in the observation and assessment centre? We will look in vain at the literature for guidance. Given the numbers of children who have been seen regularly by educational psychologists in this context one might expect the sole handbook (Chazan *et al.*, 1974) to offer concrete advice. It does after all declare that 'one may expect the educational psychologist even more than in the past to contribute to the preliminary social enquiries made by the local authority and presented in court in a written report' (p. 53).

The chapter on the reporting of psychological findings has a specific section on 'reporting to courts', which suggests a range of possible goals for the psychological investigations:

Magistrates . . . look for help and guidance from their special advisers. Basically they want some evidence to show whether a child can be helped by remaining in his own environment with, e.g. support from a social services social worker or treatment by a child guidance clinic team, or whether some other supportive action should be considered. In addition they want to know whether there are grounds for removing the child from the family altogether, and placing him in the care of the local authority, and perhaps some suggestion as the the degree of care that the authority should consider. The social services department itself may want some guidance on what to do when a child comes into care. Should the social workers, e.g. seek placement in a community home which caters for mixed handicap, or in a school for maladjusted children, and so on (*ibid* p. 265).

But from what basis of specialized knowledge the educational psychologist is to provide these answers, what form of 'assessment' will supply this information, this book does not say. What it does say is that because a disproportionate number of young offenders come from disadvantaged environments they tend to have lower than average IQs, though it has already cautioned that IQ itself is not a significant factor in producing delinquent behaviour (p. 246). Williams' (1977) more recent monograph on the ways in which educational psychologists work with children also makes no mention of the state of the art of assessment for the juvenile courts.

There have been no papers published in the profession's own journal (*Journal of the Association of Educational Psychologists*) on this topic. Brown and Sawyer (1978) in a review of the literature found scant evidence of background literature in their review of educational psychologist's work of any sort for social services departments. They note that what most psychologists do in the social service settings is to become involved in assessing individual children either before or after they appear in court on charges of delinquent activity, but that no evidence has been adduced to identify any functional benefits resulting from this. The discounting of IQ as a relevant factor in the backgrounds of delinquents (such as by Chazan *et al.*, 1974) has been the conventional wisdom for a considerable time now, but a recent reanalysis of the data available on this topic suggests that there may indeed exist a complex, mediated relationship between measured intelligence and delinquency (Hirschi and Hindelang, 1977). Consideration of IQ, therefore, in the evaluation and investigation of delinquent children represents either an exceedingly up-to-date understanding of the field, or an exceedingly out-of-date one.

Brookes (1977) has described the work of the Essex School Psychological Service in the observation and assessment centre. He reported that all children in observation and assessment centres in Essex were assessed by an educational psychologist, and that as numbers of children entering the centres had increased so the authority had increased the number of psychologists. All children were given IQ tests, reading tests and personality tests. This it is claimed gave an overall view of the problems of the children and of the schools in the various areas of the County.

There have been no further published accounts of how educational psychologists might set about investigating the children who are their clients in this particular context, or what other activities they participate in within the juvenile justice/social services nexus. They have made no apparent contributions from this practice base to the criminological or child welfare literature, nor with one exception published any other research. The exception (Whittaker, 1977) is a statistical analysis of the results of reading and intelligence tests administered at Aycliffe Assessment Centre (ex-classifying school).

From our search of the literature, then, there appears no immediate knowledge-base as manifest in the conventional form of textbooks and journal articles, to which educational psychologists can relate their fairly extensive juvenile court practice. Of course it could be that they meet the novel challenges of their work by the flexible adaptation of models and approaches from other areas of their work, or in default of this restrict their contribution carefully to matters strictly related to the educational problems for which they are experienced and trained. But if they do consult published information, then mental measurement is likely to loom large in their consciousness.

The BPS Division of Educational and Child Psychology enquiry (Wedell and Lambourne, 1979) has catalogued the frequent demands of many practising educational psychologists to operate in other roles than the conventional 'test-bashers'. This same point is reflected in a recent review of a local authority school psychological service. Topping (1978) asked a number of practitioners and a large sample of their clients to rate activities of educational psychologists, both actual and intended, real and fantasized. While educational psychologists all favoured the research – consultative items in favour of the individual testing activity, most *consumers* saw it the other way round. They wanted the educational psychologists to continue providing the IQ test results, and school heads, for example, as one of the groups sampled, wanted their educational psychologists to do the 'test-bashing' job (whether they expressed satisfaction with its usefulness or not). We need to be aware that there is an interactive, expectation effect, so that having created a mode of working, educational psychologists may be constrained from changing, not only by their own traditions, but also by the expectations of others.

Studies of Practice

To supplement the sparse literature and to investigate how indeed the lack of a knowledge base affected practice the results of three small studies are presented here. The first of these studies (Cooper, 1975) was conducted by a postgraduate student under the supervision of one of us (AS). It concerned the quality of psychological work undertaken for the Birmingham juvenile court by educational psychologists from the local education authority. At the time of this study (1974–1975) all the nine social services departments in the West Midlands Regional Planning Area had established, or were in the process of establishing, links with their local education authorities for the sessional provision of educational psychologists to their observation and assessment centres. Enquiry was made of seven educational psychologists. Their pattern of work varied, but all reported that at times they 'assessed' the children with no other background information on them than their date of birth and a statement of their offence. They always discussed the children with the staff of the centres (particularly the superintendants and the teachers), occasionally contacted the social workers, but very rarely met the parents. An interview with the child was the common feature of all their investigations, in certain cases the only feature. The only agreement amongst them about what they were 'assessing' was on the possible need for special educational placement. Administration of the *WISC* was routine practice in all cases. The psychologists felt that their unique contribution was a different 'view' of the children seen. Apart from occasional informal discussions with staff on general topics they made no other contribution to the assessment procedure. For the most part children were only 'seen' once before a report was written. Despite the explicitly 'educational' emphasis of these educational psychologists' investigations, specific examination of educational aspects of the children's academic development appeared generally limited to administration of Burt's *Graded Word Reading Test*. Their work included no research dimension. Cooper's summary view of the psychologist's contributions was that their reports were based on 'a hurried assessment of intellectual skills'. Cooper (a trainee psychologist at the time of her investigation) was exceedingly critical of the whole theoretical basis of residential observation and assessment, and almost the only dissenting voice to appear in print in the heyday of the great expansion of these centres (Cooper, 1976). The only two other educational psychologists to have contributed to this general debate have been more generally in favour of this procedure in principle (Brookes, 1977; Clayton, 1979), though in the latter case looking for improvements in their operation.

Another enquiry (Sutton, 1976) sought to identify what senior assessment centre staff thought about psychologists' contributions to the observation and assessment process. A course, now discontinued, giving in-service training for senior observation and assessment staff, provided a convenient group who would have had practical experience of working with psychologists, and some formal introduction to the theoretical questions of observation and assessment (this was the only such course in the country). The 12 staff involved came from establishments throughout the West Midlands Region and were interviewed as a group during the second term of their day-release course. The object of the group interview was to establish how the commonly agreed subculture of this relatively sophisticated collection of observation and assessment staff defined the contribution of psychologists. It is interesting that they tended to regard 'educational psychologist' and 'psychologist' as synonymous. At the end of considerable discussion the 12 agreed that the following statement represented a fair summary of their consensus view of the psychologist's role:

The psychologist, typically a LEA educational psychologist, sees children individually to administer a standardised intelligence test; apart from the results of this rating he may also contribute some practical advice on the subject of a child's education or school placement, and give some general opinion on the child based on his personal views or experience, but these contributions are not to be routinely expected; in isolated cases he might involve himself in a child's behaviour in the centre, offer information on previous contact with a child in a child guidance setting or involve himself in a child's future education; he may have some access to the mysteries claimed by the psychiatrist, at least to the extent of being able to pick out children who might require more esoteric exploration; but primarily he is an intelligence-tester, mainly relevant to the school aspects of the child's life. (Sutton, 1976, p. 4)

In return the 12 were offered an account of the psychologist as a scientist. It was not an icon that they recognized.

Aspects of these Midlands enquiries have been repeated (by GM) to see whether the same features of practice are apparent at a somewhat later date and in another part of the country.

We looked at all the psychologist's reports that had been prepared for the juvenile courts over the last 12 months, held in observation and assessment centres of a local authority. Over that period about one-third of the children passing through this observation and assessment system were there for reports for the courts. Of these only 18 per cent were actually seen and reported on to the court by an educational psychologist. The average age was 12 years, boys outnumbering girls two to one. We could not discern any explicit principle to determine who saw an educational psychologist and who did not, except that the majority of the assessed children were in the observation and assessment centres under Interim Care Orders in part at least to do with nonattendance at school.

We categorized the psychologists' reports according to common elements. Firstly, what investigations did the psychologist make? In all cases they administered all or part of an intelligence test, usually the *WISC*, occasionally the *Stanford–Binet*; one gave parts of the new *British Ability Scales*. No reasons were ever given why information about the child's IQ was sought, and no direct conclusions ever drawn from the results, apart from in the case of a mentally handicapped child where the cognitive assessment led directly to appropriate special school placement. This was the only direct link that we found between assessment and outcome.

The next most frequently investigated area was the child's reading. As we had found in the Birmingham study 5 years previously, the majority used Burt's *Graded Word Reading Test* (only one used the modern standardization), though other reading test measures were used. The most commonly drawn conclusion from this part of the assessment was of the child's educational backwardness. Sometimes unevidenced inferences were made from this about the child's likely behaviour at school, for example 'It is likely that he produces little motivation to succeed in school, as can be seen from his poor reading attainment'.

None of the psychologists involved had made use of what are usually called 'personality tests', such as had been recommended at the British Psychological Society's Division of Educational and Child Psychology seminar on the 'Developing Role of Psychology in Relation to Social Services Departments' in 1978. These would include older-style personality scales (for example, Eysenck's or Cattell's), projective procedures (for example, the *Object Relations Test* or *TAT*), self-evaluations (for example, Roger's *PI*), and family relations procedures (the *Bene–Anthony FRT*), or more up-to-date experimental methods such as repertory grid or semantic differential. We point these out not to advocate the necessary validity or relevance of such techniques in this context, but rather to point up the absence from practice of a wide range of approaches some of which at least must have been represented in all the educational psychologists' professional training. We found that these educational psychologists made no reference to formal assessment techniques other than the IQ and reading tests. Perhaps they would claim that they relied upon their 'clinical interpretations of an unstructured interview'. Certainly they drew conclusions and made recommendations on the basis of something or other, not apparent from the IQ or RA measure or from any other recorded data. The following examples of comments taken from their reports to the court we have selected as being representative of the sort of opinion offered.

(a)   On a child appearing before the court because of theft, and where no problems in school had been noted;

Investigation: Wechsler Intelligence Scale for Children.

Conclusion: 'He has a good IQ'.

Recommendation: 'He should be able to cope with regular school'.

(b)   On a 12-year-old girl who, according to her social worker, was refusing to return home because of ill-treatment and was on a place of safety order.

Investigation: Full IQ test, reading test, 'rapport with educational psychologist.'

Conclusion: 'She has adequate warmth to relate well in a supportive setting.'

Recommendation: 'Needs help soon to develop normally.'

(c)   On an 11-year-old boy, due to appear in court for theft.
      Investigation: *WISC* and reading test.
      Conclusion: 'He impresses as a child who is not accustomed to talking
      trustingly to adults.'
      Recommendation to the Court: To send him to an Observation and
      Assessment Centre under an interim Care Order for a period of further
      assessment, plus 'I have doubts as to whether X would settle into a
      Comprehensive School.' (The outcome was that X was sent to an O and
      A Centre where he was given further IQ and reading tests, then was
      placed in a family group home from where he attended the local Com-
      prehensive School).

The typical psychologist's report was one that rarely made any reference to
the *reasons* for the assessment (perhaps the educational psychologist was not
really clear about them anyway), that gave willy-nilly an IQ test and nearly
always a reading test, that drew conclusions rarely related to these enquiries,
and made recommendations that were either so vague and imprecise as to be
meaningless or else echoes of what the observation and assessment staff, social
worker, etc. had already produced. We found *no* recommendations that disagreed with the centre assessment. Moreover, when asked, none of the observation and assessment superintendents could recall an educational psychologist's ever having written any such dissenting reports for the court.

Is there indeed such an unambiguous body of knowledge, for such unequi-
vocal agreement? Or is the educational psychologist well aware of the opinions
of the observation and assessment staff, social workers etc., and of the
considerable social pressures to conform? Yet the same observation and
assessment staff said they valued the educational psychologist's contribution:
'it adds another perspective', 'it confirms our own opinion', or 'we like to have
an outside opinion'.

Enquiry about the system of feedback of outcome to the educational psychologists revealed no cases where such a system was routinely operated. Once
the educational psychologist had completed his assessment and prepared his
report to the court, he rarely discovered the outcome. While it would be
possible for the educational psychologist to discover what the juvenile court
actually did with the child, there was no system to tell the educational
psychologist what the long-term consequences were. In other words, was the
recommendation appropriate? In the absence of this feedback how can learning take place? Few if any educational psychologists are involved in work with
young offenders *after* as well as before the court hearing, and so are not in a
position to make connections between recommended treatment and outcome.

Clinical Psychologists

A very few clinical psychologists, but still rather more than educational psychologists, have become interested in the *treatment* of juvenile delinquents. While there is nothing published by educational psychologists about treatment in this context, there have been some new developments by clinical psychologists. It is not our place to describe those here, other than to point out that while one branch of psychology is involved in assessment, another is involved in the treatment of the same group of young people. This assessment–treatment dichotomy was pointed out by the DECP enquiry (Wedell and Lambourne, 1979): in most branches of child psychology, while educational psychologists were increasingly becoming involved in assessment, clinical psychologists were becoming involved in treatment. Within the juvenile court system not only is this psychometric assessment role of limited practical value, but it is also costly. Brown and Sawyer (1978) estimated its cost three years ago as around £15–18 per educational assessment a child.

There are descriptions of alternative strategies to be found, but these are the work of *clinical* psychologists in treatment. For example, Brown (1977) has described the establishing and monitoring of an intensive behaviour modification unit for highly disturbed delinquent boys, Teare (1977) the development of social skills training programmes and job preparation schemes for older delinquent youths, and Spence (1977) a project for training residential care staff in a community home in social skills training.

Conclusions

Juvenile courts in England and Wales over the last couple of decades have been the subject of widespread public debate and innovative legislation and practice. Rightly or wrongly there is now increasing public concern over some of the outcomes of changes that have been introduced. Over the past few years the largest branch of applied psychology in this country, namely the educational psychologists working for local education authorities, have arranged a close working involvement with the new system established to process children through the juvenile courts. The results of this have not been impressive in advancing either psychological knowledge or the administration of justice.

There may exist, perhaps even in considerable numbers, educational psychologists who have undertaken innovatory projects and made significant changes in the local juvenile justice systems with which they work, but no such work has as yet been published. There are certainly individual psychologists who have been highly dissatisfied with the problems and inadequacies that they have met in this context, and who have taken an alternative route; they have worked under hierarchies sufficiently flexible or sufficiently lax to permit their withdrawing altogether from this work. And there are certainly educational psychologists who have taken a third course. They have been unable or unwilling to innovate, and unable or unwilling to withdraw; instead they have stayed in and produced mediocre and derivative work.

We cannot pretend that the data that we have advanced here offers a definitive account of the national pattern of educational psychologists' extensive contribution to the juvenile courts, although it does point in a disturbingly consistent direction and does seem to accord with the experience of many practitioners on both legal and welfare sides of the juvenile court process.

We believe that mediocre practice in this field can be characterized as follows. The educational psychologist has imported into juvenile court work, primarily through the observation and assessment centres, a form of work and an ethos which is already outdated in the education system in which it has its roots. This outmoded psychological tradition is predominantly intrapsychic in orientation, psychometric in its methodology, and intellective (rather than affective) in its specific focus. To put it crudely, a child has a problem, he is 'seen' by a psychologist, and 'has his marbles counted'. What is worse, this mystifying intervention may then be used as the basis for sweeping judgements about quite unrelated areas of the child's life, which are perhaps quite outside the psychologist's personal experience or technical competence. Such mediocre practice undoubtedly exists, a major question is what proportion does it constitute of the whole?

Another major question is, where is the good practice? Juvenile delinquency and other problems that come before the juvenile court involve countless important human conditions crying out for decent psychological involvement and research. It can be argued that there is something fundamentally unethical about a psychologist's working in an area conspicuous by the absence of knowledge, and *not* doing research. But in this area, as in others, educational psychologists seem rather cut off from the research process, both as producers and as consumers (c.f. Quick, 1979; Hart and Taylor, 1979) and thus from the basis of psychology as a whole.

Psychologists and others (see Sheldon, 1981) may have good cause to deprecate some of the psychological 'knowledge' of social workers. But if indeed a significant proportion of the direct application of psychology to the juvenile courts is itself of poor quality, then one cannot blame the others involved for their psychologies. Worse than this, psychology as a whole is in danger of being discredited.

Notes

1 'Educational psychologists' is a particularly British term. The more general international term is 'school psychologists'.
2 The case is different in Scotland.

Statutes

1838 An Act for Establishing a Prison for Young Offenders
1847 An Act for the More Speedy Trial and Punishment of Juvenile Offenders
1879 Summary Jurisdiction Act
1908 Children's Act
1933 Children and Young Persons Act
1969 Children and Young Persons Act

References

Brookes, B. (1977), 'The psychologist in social services assessment', *Essex Education*, **31**, 3, 11.

Brown, B. J. (1977), 'Gilbey House: a token economy management scheme in a residential school for adolescent boys in trouble', *B.A.B.P. Bulletin*, **5**, 3, 79.

Brown, B. J. and Sawyer, C. E. (1978), 'Uses and abuses of psychologists – some alternatives for psychologists working in social services departments', *Bulletin of the British Psychological Society*, **31**, 218.

Burt, C. (1925), *The Young Delinquent*, London University Press.

Chazan, M., Moore, T., Williams, P. and Wright, J. (1974), *The Practice of Educational Psychology*, Longman, Harlow.

Clayton, T. (1979), 'Residential observation and assessment under attack', *Journal of the Association of Educational Psychologists*, **5**, 38.

Cooper, P. (1975), 'Social services departments' observation and assessment centres of children', University of Birmingham unpublished MEd dissertation.

Cooper, P. (1976), 'Why residential assessment?', in Hughes, M. (ed.), *Observation and Assessment – A Changing Concept*, Selly Oak Colleges, Birmingham.

Gillham, B. (ed.) (1978), *Reconstructing Educational Psychology*, Croom Helm. London.

Hart, D. and Taylor, A. (1979), 'Publications by educational psychologists', *Occasional Papers, Division of Educational and Child Psychology, British Psychological Society*, **3**, 1, 28.

Hirschi, T. and Hindelang, M. J. (1977), 'Intelligence and delinquency: a revisionist review', *American Sociological Review*, **42**, 571.

Hoghughi, M. (1979), 'Myth, method and utility', *Social Work Today*, **10**, 29, 11.

Porteous, M. (1978), 'Psychologists working in social services departments', *Bulletin of the British Psychological Society*, **31**, 298.

Quick, J. (1979), 'The professional knowledge of educational psychologists', *Journal of the Association of Educational Psychologists*, **4**, 8.

Sheldon, B. (1981), 'Psychology and social work', in Brown, M. and Muir, L. (eds), *Social Work Practice: A Basic Text*, Macmillan, Basingstoke.

Spence, S. (1977), 'An investigation into the effectiveness of social skills training in improving social interaction performance with adolescent offenders or potential offenders', unpublished manuscript, Tennal School, Birmingham.

Summerfield, A. (ed.) (1968), *Psychologists in Education Services*, HMSO, London.

Sutton, A. (1976), 'The role of the psychologist in social service departments' observation and assessment centres', unpublished manuscript.

Sutton, A. (1978), 'Fact, fantasy and educational psychologists', *Bulletin of the British Psychological Society*, **31**, 423.

Teare, P. (1977), 'Teaching social skills to delinquent adolescents', in Jarman, R. M. (ed.) *Behavioural Approaches to the Treatment of Delinquent Adolescents*, unpublished manuscript, Tennal School, Birmingham.

Topping, K. J. (1978), 'Consumer confusion and professional conflict in educational psychology', *Bulletin of the British Psychological Society*, **31**, 265.

Ward, E. S. (1978), 'On a point of evidence', *Bulletin of the British Psychological Society*, **31**, 8.

Watson, J. A. F. (1942), *The Child and the Magistrate*, Jonathan Cape.

Wedell, K. and Lambourne, R. (1979), *An Enquiry into Psychological Services for Children in England and Wales*, University of Birmingham, Faculty of Education.

Whittaker, E. M. (1977), 'Aspects of intellectual and educational functioning of boys admitted to a regional assessment centre', *Journal of the Association of Educational Psychologists*, **4**, 24.

Williams, P. (1977), *Psychologists and Children*, Longman, London.

Problems of the Clinical Psychologist as Expert Witness

ERIC WARD*

This paper discusses briefly the main problems of the clinical psychologist in providing expert evidence. These arise from: (i) lack of facilities; (ii) lack of training opportunities; (iii) the control of information; (iv) lack of clinical procedures appropriate to legal questions; (v) confidentiality of reports; and (vi) communication and the use of information. I will define a 'clinical psychologist' as a psychologist who has a postgraduate qualification in clinical psychology recognized by the Division of Clinical Psychology of the British Psychological Society. The majority of clinical psychologists are employed in the National Health Service principally in the fields of mental illness, mental handicap, and the various children's services for example child psychiatric units and paediatric units, etc. There has also been in recent years an increasing involvement in general medical services at both a hospital and general practitioner level. Additionally, it is anticipated that clinical psychologists will provide services to the proposed 'intermediate secure units' being built by the Regional Health Authorities. While the clinical psychologist's job description includes teaching, research and management functions a significant proportion of their work is still concerned with the assessment and treatment of individual patients. This will often be in the context of a multidisciplinary team, comprising psychologists, psychiatrists, nurses, and possibly others. In addition, all but a minority of hospital psychology departments will accept direct referrals from a general practitioner or social work department. Only a small proportion of the patients referred to a psychology department are likely to be involved in legal proceedings. Unfortunately, departments do not keep statistical records of the number of referrals involving legal proceedings as a proportion of the total referrals. Therefore, no hard data is available. However, one would expect the proportion to be higher in those hospitals which offer specialist alcohol, drug addiction or intermediate secure units, particularly if the latter are developed into a Regional Forensic Service.

*Lecturer in Psychology, Institute of Psychiatry, London.

Lack of Facilities

This applies both to the provision of specialized forensic services within the Health Service, and to the provision of psychological services in general. Despite the protestations of good intent by various governments few steps have actually been taken in providing specialist forensic services in the Health Service. This is reflected in the availability of clinical psychological services, and therefore in the willingness of psychologists to undertake court work. As psychology departments do not themselves have access to hospital beds, any services they offer to the court must be capable of being performed on an out-patient basis or by visiting the patient at his place of residence, which may of course be a prison. That is not to say that an individual psychologist may not have made arrangements with a particular consultant for the latter to admit the patient to one of his own beds, or for both psychiatrist and psychologist to be involved from the outset so that the psychiatrist admits the patient to one of his beds. It may be singularly unhelpful for the psychologist to make recommendations to the court on the patient's suitability for treatment if he lacks the facility to carry them out. Lack of facilities may also pose limitations on the type of assessment the psychologist can carry out and hence on the type of evidence he can present to the court.

Lack of Training Opportunities

The limited facilities available and the absence of suitably experienced psychologists have placed limitations on the training opportunities available at a postgraduate level. Few courses can offer more than basic teaching in forensic psychology, and I know of only three that give any instruction in how to prepare evidence for court proceedings. Opportunities for actual court experience are even more limited. A number of training courses have attempted to offer some experience with forensic patients by arranging placements in the special hospitals or in one case at a local prison. One hopes that with the development of Regional Forensic Services, a wider clinical experience and adequate instruction, including experience of court work can be arranged.

Control of Information

The psychologist is often unaware that his report is being used as evidence in court, as psychological evidence is often *not* given by the *psychologist* himself but is included by the *psychiatrist* in his medical report. This is despite the fact that the psychologist's assessment may be the lynch-pin on which the report hangs. The court and the psychologist may both be unaware from the wording of the report that this has occurred. The original psychological report may have been prepared at the patient's admission, or as part of a rehabilitation programme and then placed in the patient's case notes. Once the report has been placed in the case notes it is easily accessible to any member of staff and the psychologist has no control over any use that may be made of the information. There are a number of objections to this practice:

(1) The psychiatrist is presenting 'hearsay' evidence which should not be admitted in criminal proceedings. This point has often been made before (for example, Haward, 1965; Ward, 1978).

(2) As the psychiatrist's qualifications are in psychiatry and not in psychology, it may be argued that he is not a 'competent' witness to give evidence as an expert witness in psychology.

(3) The *Current Guidelines for the Professional Practice of Clinical Psychologists* issued by the Division of Clinical Psychology of the British Psychological Society emphasizes the additional care that should be taken when communicating a psychologist's findings to non-psychologists. It is impossible to do this when the psychologist has no control over the channel of communication.

(4) In quoting from the psychologist's report the psychiatrist is usually selective in the information he includes. This process may result in a significantly different communication from that intended by the psychologist.

(5) The procedures used in the original investigation may be unsuitable for the purposes that the court wishes to use them. This may not be immediately apparent to either the court or the psychiatrist.

(6) As the original psychological report was not prepared with the court's objectives in mind, pertinent information may have been omitted from the report as irrelevant to the original purposes of the investigation.

These points are not of academic interest alone. The author was recently involved in a civil action following a road accident. The severely injured plaintiff had passed through a rehabilitation unit and the psychologist at that unit had described him as having a mild memory dysfunction. The defendants argued that as the deficit was only a mild one he was capable of employment; on the other hand the plaintiff's advisers argued that the reverse was the case. On neither side did the neurologists advising counsel for each party seem to understand the psychological assessment. The assessment was in fact a brief report prepared for internal use within the hospital in the context of a particular rehabilitation programme and unsuitable for the use that was being made of it. It was necessary to carry out a new set of assessments and a more detailed investigation to answer counsel's questions. Lawyers often seem to forget that psychology is not a medical sub-speciality.

Lack of Clinical Procedures Appropriate to Legal Qestions

As an expert witness the psychologist often faces the difficulty that the instru-
ments and procedures available to him sometimes do not match the questions
the court has set. For instance, in R-v-P, a Crown Court case, the defendant
had confessed to theft, and the defence maintained that he was mentally
handicapped and that his confession therefore was unreliable. It was comparatively easy to establish his level of intellectual functioning; on the Wechsler Adult Intelligence Scale he had an IQ of 70, and during his childhood had
attended an ESN school. However, to demonstrate that his testimony was
therefore unreliable is another matter. As a psychologist I know of no experimental evidence which demonstrates that the confession of such a person is
necessarily unreliable, or that the reliability of confessions is significantly
correlated with intelligence. It may be that the confessions of both normal and
mentally handicapped subjects are unreliable. Alterntively, it may be that a
certain percentage of the confessions of normal people and a similar percentage of the confessions of the mentally handicapped are unreliable due to some
factor other than intelligence. If this is so, the spectacular cases which have
resulted in the Home Office Guidelines are a sub-set of the confessions made
by the mentally handicapped. Unfortunately, no research appears to have
been carried out to clarify this area.

The clinical psychologist is therefore forced to rely on less substantial
clinical observations, such as the subject's responses to test items to which he
does not know the answers. Does the subject persistently construct answers
when he does not have a clue what the correct answer is, or does he become
silent and morose? This procedure raises problems of validity and generalizability. Do the observations being made actually answer the questions they
are purporting to answer, and even if they do can the information obtained in
the assessment be applied to the subject's behaviour under interrogation?
While the objective of psychological research is to produce results which
elucidate parameters that are valid and that can be generalized from one
situation to another this must be demonstrated by investigation and cannot be
assumed a priori. But again, the necessary research has not been done. While it
would seem likely that those people who perform in such a manner on testing
would also do so in interrogation, there may well be a sample who are not
easily influenced in testing but who would be so influenced in an interrogation.
An interesting discussion of interrogation from a decision-making viewpoint
and the factors that influence it, is offered by Hilgendorf and Irving (1981). In
the particular case of R-v-P it was fortunate for the defendant that prosecuting
counsel had not read Ziskin (1975) or he would have drawn the court's
attention to such problems. Psychologists to date have done little to provide

the information to meet this need and given the present economic conditions are unlikely to do so in the foreseeable future.

In those situations in which established procedures are available to answer the court's questions there can still be problems. In R-v-H, another Crown Court case, the defendant was alleged to have read and signed a confession but then claimed to his solicitors that he was illiterate. Unfortunately, while accurate and reliable measures of reading ability are available, they have invariably been standardized on children and have a maximum age range of 16 years. They have not been standardized on devious and experienced criminals who have a vested interest in obtaining the lowest score they can. Prosecuting counsel was able to point out that such tests should have been standardized on persons such as the defendant if they are to be applied to him. In practice, all one can do is to use a variety of tests with different scoring systems which would require different and conflicting strategies if they were to be faked. But such a point is complex and difficult to present succinctly to a jury. In my opinion, the only way H could have faked the tests would have resulted in either a zero score or different scores on different tests. As the defendant was on remand in Brixton prison before trial he is unlikely to have had prior access to the test materials in order to create a strategy for faking them.

The problem of confessions made by mentally handicapped patients highlights our lack of knowledge at the interface of law and clinical psychology. The Home Office guidelines state:

The Home Secretary thinks it desirable that, so far as is practicable, and where recognised as such by the police, a mentally handicapped adult (whether suspected of a crime or not) should be interviewed only in the presence of a parent or other person in whose care, custody or control he is, or of some person who is not a police officer (for example a social worker).

The guidelines make the presumption that the presence of such a third party will reduce the likelihood of a false confession. It may prevent overt threats or physical abuse, but I have seen no evidence that it would affect the more subtle forms of behavioural influence. From social psychology experiments one would expect the effect to depend on such factors as perceived status, non-verbal cues, and the type of role adopted by the third party. If the social worker were to adopt a compliant, acquiescent role she could be perceived as a 'compliant model' and reduce the subject's ability to resist the police interviewer, thereby increasing the probability of a false confession. The most significant point, however, is that the guidelines have been introduced without any experimental investigation of any effects they may or may not have.

Confidentiality

Problems can also arise for the clinical psychologist when he is treating patients who are themselves defendants in criminal proceedings. One of the major problems is that of confidentiality, in that the patient may have given information to the psychologist in confidence which he would be very reluctant to admit in court. For example, when treating an exhibitionist one would collect considerable information from him on all his sexual activities, including those which may not be the subject of proceedings. If faced with direct questions in the witness box the psychologist would have a choice between disclosure and perjury. On the other hand if the patient is not free to discuss such matters with the psychologist the possibility of treatment is non-existent. The problem becomes particularly acute when the patient has himself sought treatment before contact with the police and the information relates to that period. The difficulty remains even if such offences are 'taken into consideration'. A similar problem exists for the medical profession, but both society and to a lesser extent the courts recognize this and are reluctant to force such testimony from the witness box. At least one American state has granted a privilege status to communications between a psychologist and his client. This would be one logical solution to the present dilemma, but one which is unlikely to find favour with the English judiciary.

Communication and the Use of Information

A further problem emerges when one considers the way in which information is used by the psychologist on the one hand and by the courts on the other. The psychologist will have only one type of model available to him – a therapeutic one – and this will be easily apparent to the court. (In practice the situation will be complicated in that different psychologists will use different therapeutic models.) But it will not be clear to the psychologist whether the court will be acting in a therapeutic manner (for example, making a probation order with a condition of treatment); or out of a desire to protect the public; or with a view to punishing the individual; or even with the aim of making him an example to others. The courts may choose any one of a number of different models when processing the information given to them by a psychologist, and in disposal of the defendent if he is found guilty. The psychologist has to rely on defence counsel to make an uninspired guess! Is it ethical for a psychologist to present to a court operating on a punitive model information supplied to him in confidence at a time when both he and the client were operating on a therapeutic model? This is a particularly acute problem since contemporary practice requires that the psychologist keep detailed reports and records of his client's problem which, if exposed to a court, are potentially far more damaging than conventional psychiatric records. On the other hand, if they are withheld he may be unable to present the most powerful evidence available to him. Such records may document for example a 40 per cent or even a 75 per cent improvement in the client's condition, but if treated unsympathetically indicate a greater degree of delinquency than the handful of offences listed on the charge sheet.

If the psychologist in his evidence suggests to the court that a particular form of treatment is appropriate, the court at present may either permit the treatment on a voluntary basis or make such treatment a condition of a probation order. There is no equivalent procedure to the Mental Health Act 1959 Sections for compulsory treatment by a psychologist. At present the court would have to make an order with the co-operation of a psychiatrist, and on the understanding that a particular psychologist would then provide the treatment. This would appear to be a rather antiquated and cumbersome procedure; it would be simpler if the order could have been made to the psychologist in the first place. This would require two changes, the first in existing legislation and the second in Health Service practise, to permit a non-medical practitioner (that is, a psychologist) to have access to hospital beds. Both changes would, no doubt, attract considerable opposition from the medical profession.

The difficulties posed by the lack of facilities and of training opportunities will hopefully improve with establishment of Regional Forensic Services, and the increasing contact between clinical psychologists and the legal professions. This will enable more effective training programmes to be developed. Unfortunately, problems related to the control of information cannot be solved by the clinical psychologist because once his report is placed in the patient's case notes it is accessible to almost anyone and the psychologist has no control over the use that might be made of it. Control must, therfore, be exercized through the courts under the normal rules of evidence. Unfortunately, counsel appear to be reluctant to challenge medical evidence on this point.

The problems of communication of information, obtained in a clinical setting to a court which may use any of several different models appears to be as intractable as most ethical issues. It seems unlikely that a satisfactory solution can be reached although clarification of the issues involved would make a fruitful area of discussion for both lawyers and psychologists. I have left till last the question of the applicability of available clinical data to legal problems as it enables me to conclude on a more optimistic note, for many of the questions are capable of an answer – providing, of course, that adequate financial resources are made available and the political will to find solutions exists. It would, for example, be quite feasible to test the Home Office Guidelines, or to investigate the effects of IQ on confessions.

References

British Psychological Society (1974), *Current Guidelines for the Professional Practice of Clinical Psychology*.

Haward, L. R. C. (1965), 'Hearsay and psychological evidence,' *Bulletin of the British Psychological Society*, **18**, 58.

Hilgendorf, E. L. and Irving, B. (1981), 'A decision making model of confessions', in Lloyd-Bostock, S. M. A. (ed.), *Psychology in Legal Contexts*, Macmillan, London.

Ward, E. S. (1978), 'On a point of evidence.' *Bulletin of the British Psychological Society*, **31**, 8–10.

Ziskin, J. (1975), *Coping with Psychiatric and Psychological Testimony*, Law and Psychology Press (2nd Edn.).

Antidiscrimination Legislation and the Role of the Social Sciences*

CHRISTOPHER McCRUDDEN†

There are three main questions I want to examine:
(i) Why are social science issues involved in what appears at first sight a rather narrow issue of definition: the meaning of racial and sexual discrimination?
(ii) In what ways might social science methodology and social scientists contribute to decision-making in this area?
(iii) In view of the fact that it is largely because of American developments (both legal and social scientific) that these issues arise in British legislation, how has the USA's experience been translated into the British context?

Social Science and American Anti-discrimination Law

Social science and social scientists were involved at each stage of those American developments though in starkly contrasting roles. Four phases of relationship between the social sciences and antidiscrimination law in the USA may be identified.

In the first, until the 1930s, social science may be seen as having been a supporter of racism and an opponent of attempts to remedy discrimination. Of all the examples that might be given, the one which perhaps best illustrates this relationship is the case of *Plessy v. Ferguson*[1] in 1896 in which a state law which segregated blacks and whites in railway cars was under constitutional challenge in the US Supreme Court. The influence of the fledgling social sciences can be seen throughout the opinion which Justice Brown delivered,

---

*This is a preliminary attempt to address the issues. It is one part of continuing work on the development of anti-discrimination legislation in the United Kingdom and the USA.

†Balliol College, Oxford.

upholding the law. In one particularly remarkable part of the opinion he wrote:

We consider the underlying fallacy of the plaintiff's argument to consist in the assumption that the enforced separation of the two races stamps the coloured race with a badge of inferiority. If this be so, it is not by reason of anything found in the act, but solely because the coloured race chooses to put that construction upon it. (p. 551)

Perhaps the reader will agree with Professor Black's comment on this 'psychological' analysis that, 'The curves of callousness and stupidity intersect at their respective maxima.' (Black, 1959, p. 422). Later in the opinion, Justice Brown entones:

Legislation is powerless to eradicate racial instincts or to abolish distinctions based upon physical differences . . . If the civil and political rights of both races be inferior to the other socially, the Constitution of the United States cannot put them upon the same plane. (pp. 551–552)

In the second phase, beginning before World War II, social science contributed to the destruction of the scientific basis of racism – a destruction which was hastened by evidence of the Nazi holocaust, itself an example of 'scientific racism'. In the USA a growing number of sociologists and psychologists among others reexamined the problems of race and refocused the debate from 'what is wrong with the blacks' to 'what is wrong with the whites'. Myrdal (1944) in *An American Dilemma*, and Adorno, Frenkel-Brunswik, Levinson and Sanford (1950) in *The Authoritarian Personality* are of course the outstanding examples of this type of work.

By the beginning of the 1950s, can be seen the development of the third phase in the relationship. Social science becomes a supportive component of the struggle to remedy and prevent racial discrimination. There were perhaps two ways in which social science contributed. First, no doubt also influenced by the interventionist New Deal, social scientists contested and eventually overcame the Sumnerian proposition, that 'law-ways' cannot change 'folk-ways' (Sumner, 1907; c.f. Vann Woodward, 1966, pp. 102–104). A new orthodoxy took its place which argued that the law *could* successfully intervene to change at least behaviour, if not opinion. Second, social science contributed personnel and evidence to challenge, and also eventually to overcome, the popular psychology on which *Plessy* was based. The forum in which those who challenged segregation and discrimination chose (or, rather, were forced) to fight was the courts, particularly the federal courts. Segregation was challenged as being contrary to the Fourteenth Amendment of the American Constitution. The Amendment had been adopted after the American Civil

War in 1868 as part of an attempt to secure the rights of the freed slaves. It provided in part that 'No State shall . . . deny to any person within its jurisdiction the equal protection of the laws.'

The question of whether social science evidence should be introduced at all as part of the constitutional challenge to *Plessy* was an extremely divisive issue within the ranks of lawyers preparing the famous *Brown v. Board of Education*[2] case in which segregation in schools was declared unconstitutional in 1954. Eventually it *was* decided to put before the Supreme Court evidence that segregation tended to create feelings of inferiority and personal humiliation in black children, whose sense of self-esteem was soon replaced with self-hatred, rejection of their racial group, and frustration, and that anti-social and delinquent behaviour were the probable result.

This approach appears to have been successful; for in *Brown* the Supreme Court declared enforced segregation by state law to be unconstitutional under the federal Fourteenth Amendment, and in doing so made direct reference to social science evidence. Referring to the psychological premise on which *Plessy* was based, Chief Justice Warren brusquely disagreed:

Whatever may have been the extent of psychological knowledge at the time of *Plessy v. Ferguson* [the] finding [that segregation denotes inferiority and diminishes learning motivation] is amply supported by modern authority. (p. 494)

To support this brief dismissal of one of the bases of *Plessy*, Warren added what has become probably the most famous footnote of the Court's history (footnote 11) which listed seven works by contemporary social scientists, all of which had been cited by the lawyers during litigation.

In the charged atmosphere of American race relations this apparently innocuous footnote provoked sustained criticism from many, even those who agreed with the result the Court had come to, and, predictably, vitriolic attacks from those who did not. For example, Professor Edmond Cahn, a supporter of the result, disliked the impression being given that *Brown* was a matter of social science rather than a common sense application of the constitutional requirement of equal protection under the law. 'It should have been obvious all along', he wrote, 'that segregation harms'; proving this was like proving 'that fire burns', or 'that a cold causes snuffles' (Cahn, 1955, p. 161).

Despite such scepticism, the Supreme Court survived and so did their evident approval of the social science approach, though in a more muted, *sotto voce*, way. The eventual passage by Congress of the Civil Rights Acts in 1964, 1965 and 1968 gave an added dimension to the antidiscrimination role of the federal courts. From that time, not only was it possible to contest discrimination in voting rights and public education (as in *Brown*) but also in private employment and housing.

Of the many developments after *Brown* and the passage of the Civil Rights Acts, by far the most important and the one I most want to emphasise, was the development of the concept of 'institutional discrimination' in the mid- to late 1960s. Hitherto the idea of discrimination had been restricted to mean, basically, the outward manifestation of prejudice. In Britain this has been termed 'direct discrimination'. At its simplest it may be illustrated by the situation where I refuse employment to a man because he is black, and I don't like blacks. By the end of the 1960s, however, 'discrimination' was being used popularly (and often none too clearly) to refer to the *under-representation* of blacks which resulted from their underclass position in American society. No longer was it necessary, then, for someone alleging discrimination to show prejudice or even knowledge of the exclusionary effect of a policy: when the result of one's actions was to exclude blacks disproportionately, this was institutional discrimination.

The popular interpretation was embraced by the courts. This development resulted from a number of factors: for example the difficulty which plaintiffs found in proving discriminatory motive, the pernicious continuing results of overt intentional discrimination which happened in the past, and the need to do something *quickly* after the riots of the mid-1960s. In addition, however, it also, as Wolf puts it, was 'deeply related to some aspects of an over-simplified assimilationist perspective in American sociological thought . . .'. (Wolf, 1972) Again, the influence of current social scientific thinking may be seen.

In *education* cases one result of the acceptance of the notion of institutional discrimination was the greater willingness, at least of the lower federal courts, to base far-reaching remedies, including busing, upon a finding of what came to be called *de facto* discrimination, rather than the previously required *de jure* discrimination.[3] In *employment* cases the high point of this emphasis on institutional discrimination was the decision by the US Supreme Court in *Griggs v. Duke Power Co.*[4] in 1971. In that case a requirement that employees, in order to be promoted, must have attained a certain score on an occupational test as well as have a high school diploma, was struck down by the Supreme Court. Chief Justice Burger wrote that:

tests or criteria for employment or promotion may not provide equality of opportunity only in the sense of the fabled offer of milk to the stork and the fox. Congress has now required that the posture and condition of the job-seekers be taken into account. It has . . . provided that the vessel in which the milk is proffered is one all seekers can use. The Act proscribes not only overt discrimination, but also practices that are fair in form, but discriminatory in operation. The touchstone is business necessity. Good intent or absence of discriminatory intent does not redeem employment procedures or testing mechanisms that operate as 'built-in headwinds' for minority groups and are unrelated to measuring job capability.

In examining whether such occupational tests were discriminatory the Court examined evidence provided by the US Equal Employment Opportunities Commission, in the form of Guidelines which they had issued relating to such tests (EEOC, 1966, para, 1607.1). The Court, accepting their expertise, approved the guidelines. In subsequent decisions this *Griggs* approach was also applied where sex discrimination was alleged, so that the 'effects' test, as it became known, now applies in employment discrimination cases alleging race or sex discrimination. In these cases the giving of expert evidence by industrial psychologists is commonplace.

Since about 1975, however, the relationship between social science and race relations law has entered yet another phase in the USA: one in which there is growing scepticism by lawyers and judges as to the usefulness of social science in solving public policy problems in the race relations field. This scepticism has manifested itself, for example, in the unwillingness of the Supreme Court to approve, in education cases, the lower courts adoption of the *de facto* test (see Brest, 1975, pp. 530–540). It is apparent too in the refusal, in *Washington v. Davis*,[5] a case decided in 1976, to extend the *Griggs* 'effects test' to employment cases under the Fourteenth Amendment.

Discrimination and Social Science Issues in Britain

Those developing the British legislation appear to have been influenced more by the American development *prior* to 1974, however, and the British Acts throw up many issues in which American social scientists were and are involved and the examination of which might require, or at least be susceptible to, a British social science input. In particular, the idea of 'indirect discrimination' in the British Acts – a transplant of the *Griggs* case from the USA – involves issues of public policy, industrial relations, psychology, statistics and sociology of a high degree of importance and potential complexity.

Both the Sex Discrimination Act 1975 and the Race Relations Act 1976 prohibit, in particular circumstances, the use of conditions or requirements which have the effect of disproportionately excluding a particular racial (or sexual) group and which cannot be shown to be 'justifiable'. Briefly, three things have to be shown by a person alleging indirect discrimination. First (using an employment situation as an example) does the employer have a requirement for promotion which he applies to both his Pakistani and English workers, for example a requirement that they pass a language proficiency test?

Second, if so, is this requirement such that the proportion of Pakistanis able to comply with it is considerably smaller than the proportion of non-Pakistani workers able to comply with it? For example, do considerably fewer Pakistani workers pass the test than do non-Pakistani workers? Third, is the person who is actually alleging discrimination not able to comply with the requirement – the need to prove 'detriment'? (In the example of language testing, is the person who is complaining of discrimination himself not able to pass the test?) If these three elements are shown, then the employer must show that the condition is justifiable; otherwise it is found to be 'indirectly discriminatory'.

The issue is not whether decisions relating to the application of the Acts in general, and 'indirect discrimination' in particular, will be made on the basis of ideas related to these wider disciplines. They inevitably will. Rather, it is whether the interpreter will decide largely on the basis of his own received (and possibly wildly inaccurate) knowledge of those matters, or on the basis of evidence presented by social scientists with some greater degree of knowledge and expertise in the area.

Taking into account the American experience, what role might one espouse for the social sciences in this area? Kalven provides a starting point for debate in his delimitation of the proper role of social science in relation to policy making in the legal process:

Some premises are too deeply held for actual footnoting, and some facts are too well and accessibly known for professional inquiry. What remains then as the central area is the middle range where the premises are not that unshakeable and where the facts are not that accessible.

It is for this reason, I suspect, that both sides in any ideological dispute about bringing social science empiricism to law tend to overshoot the mark. On the one hand, it is simplistic to urge that because law makes factual assumptions, there should be a one-to-one linking and testing of the underlying social facts, an endless dropping of empirical footnotes to points of law. On the other hand, it is nonsense to say that better documentation of fact cannot ever be relevant to law because the final business of law is not truth but political preference (Kelven, 1968, p. 67).

The relevance of social scientific explication of social facts is, for Kalven, 'oblique'. 'They serve' he says, 'to narrow the controversy by eliminating certain points of disagreement or by suggesting unsuspected connections to other points' (p. 67).

In Britain, those representing individual complainants and the Commission for Racial Equality (CRE) or the Equal Opportunities Commission (EOC) in conducting formal investigations, may thus legitimately seek to have social scientists involved for any one or more of a number or reasons, as have litigating lawyers in the USA:

(i) to provide skills necessary in substantiating the application of a legal concept to a particular situation, for example proof of discrimination may involve both statistical and psychological expertise;

(ii) to provide evidence of 'social facts' useful in appreciating the consequences of the decision in its social context;

(iii) to supplement 'common knowledge' in order better to assess evidence given, for example whether a thing is probable or not in a given circumstance;

(iv) to legitimate and give extra weight to an argument based on value choices, for example whether a condition or requirement *prima facie* indirectly discriminatory, is nonetheless 'justifiable'.

A Sceptical Assessment of Social Science Involvement in British Antidiscrimination Law

Despite these possibilities, I remain somewhat sceptical as to any substantial future direct use of social science evidence in race or sex discrimination cases, at least to the degree accepted as normal in the USA. It seems to me much more likely that social science will, at best, be only *indirectly* utilized. My scepticism is based on these following reasons.

Low 'Rights Consciousness'

First, there are very few claims of discrimination, direct or indirect. For example, under the Sex Discrimination Act, 1975, applications alleging sex discrimination in employment to industrial tribunals in 1978 numbered 178 (HMSO, 1980, p. 384). In 1978, allegations of *direct* discrimination on grounds of sex or against married persons predominated, accounting for over 91.4 per cent of all cases of discrimination under the Act. Indirect discrimination claims amounted to only 8.6 per cent of cases (HMSO 1980, p. 384). Individual applications under the Race Relations Act show the same pattern (HMSO, 1980, p. 351; see also CRE 1978, 1979). There are even fewer non employment cases. Few cases mean little incentive to attempt an expensive and time consuming institutionalizing of social scientific expertise.

Social Scientific Culture

My second reason for scepticism is based on the British social scientific culture. In the USA (at least until recently) the social scientific culture seems to have been much more sympathetic to the involvement of social science in this area of policy making than it is in Britain. The American scientific and social scientific communities were available and willing to contribute to this involvement. The environment was right for a number of reasons. Empiricism was not only the dominant American scientific approach. It also supported and indeed was reflected in sociological jurisprudence. As Rosen (1972) points out:

In all certainty, the gradual rise of an empirically oriented jurisprudence was not an isolated cultural movement but inevitably revealed the legal facet of a cultural order thoroughly permeated with – and wholly distinguished by – empiricism. (p. 156).

Lawyers and scientists also had similar conceptions of the relationship of science to policy, that is, there was a willingness on both sides to use social science for social engineering. Thirdly, the rejection of an atomistic, and the adoption of a holistic, approach by sociological jurisprudence was also reflective of the holism of the American scientific community. Pound (1942), for example, emphasized that the developing teamwork of lawyers and 'other [sic] social sciences' is an element of 'the study of law as part of a whole process of social control. This is an essential point in the twentieth-century sociological jurisprudence' (pp. 124–125). Lastly, and perhaps most importantly, there was a general consensus on what goal was sought to be achieved.

Other secondary factors encouraged (and were encouraged by) these developments in legal and social scientific thought. One set of factors relates to the sheer availability of relevant social science evidence, particularly since the culture is one which is willing to be tabulated and researched, with personnel to do it and interpret the results. In addition, the financial resources are there to encourage, promote, publicize and support: the public interest foundations and law firms which they fund were and are a vital ingredient in a very expensive process.

In Britain I perceive much greater scepticism among British social scientists as to the utility of involving courts in the remedying of discrimination than exists among their counterparts in the USA. In particular where employment matters are concerned, the influence of 'voluntarism' is all pervasive and biased against such intervention (Flanders, 1975). There is not in Britain, while there was in the USA in the 1940s, 1950s and 1960s, a widespread acceptance by social scientists of their being actively involved in social engineering *as well as* adding to scientific knowledge. Nor is there a consensus as to what goal should be sought.

In Britain too there is much less work being done by social scientists on race or sex discrimination (even apart from the specifically socio-legal issues with which I have been mainly concerned) than is taking place in the USA. Where such work *is* being done, a further major problem is that most of it is unusable directly in a legal setting, often because there is a use of concepts, even for example 'discrimination', which may seem similar to legal concepts but which turn out to diverge widely from them. So too the results are often published in unusable form; they are macro when micro is needed, or ethnological when statistical would be more useful. As Kalven has written of the involvement of science and law generally, 'The upshot is that collation of texts will not take us very far and that if science is to help on legal problems, research will have to be done freshly' (Kalven, 1968, p. 62).

I do not want, however, to give the impression that *no* involvement is taking place. Indeed in each of the major indirect discrimination cases, social scientists have been involved. My point is less extreme. It is simply that this co-operation, while important and encouraging, may well *not* illustrate future developments and that the American empirical approach will not be securely transplanted to Britain but, rather, will remain uncertain and tentative.

A related reason for this is the extent to which, in the *future* even, relevant information will be collected in usable form. The opposition of some trade unionists to monitoring and the collection of statistical information on the basis of race in the workplace, and a similar suspicion some of those in minority groups themselves have of the general collection of such information, for example by census, may well mean that necessary information will not become available in the future. Professor McAuslan's observation in another context is equally relevant here: '. . . our political culture does not believe in or therefore facilitiate full disclosure of information, some of which might be inconvenient, and this is an essential pre-condition of a more active judiciary' (McAuslan, 1975, p. 23) – and, one might add, of a more active involvement of social scientists. It is not therefore a question of available but unused evidence, nor of large numbers of social scientists eager to enter into the legal process.

Legal Culture

My third reason for scepticism is based on the difference in legal cultures. A number of factors have contributed to ensuring that in the USA social science came to be widely accepted in an adjudicatory forum. The constitutional and Bill of Rights functions of the federal courts and the wide leeway for judicial choice which they necessarily give, contributed to the realisation of the wide range of implications of judicial decisions and a consequent eagerness to have the best information possible on which to base such decisions. Later, the move away from regarding law as an impotent and, indeed, deleterious tool for social engineering, and the resulting social legislation of the twentieth century, involved the courts in the task of interpreting and applying laws which attempted to bring about fundamental changes in the society but which also gave a large degree of discretion in how they were to be interpreted.

Both of these factors encouraged, and in turn were encouraged by, the development of sociological jurisprudence, which, in accepting and popularizing the policy-making functions of judges, actively encouraged academic and judicial interrelationships between law and the social sciences. As long ago as 1912 Roscoe Pound was writing:

> If the traditional element of the law will not hear of new ethical ideas, or will not hear of the usages of the mercantile community, or will not hear of new economics or of the tenets of the modern social sciences, legislation will long beat its unaffected wings in vain.

What was then a revolutionary view became from the 1930s the new orthodoxy, both in the better and more influential law schools and in the federal courts.

Sociological jurisprudence, in supplying empiricism as a prescriptive alternative to the pretence that judges are value neutral, thus prevented the descent into another alternative based on the proposition that judges' decisions must be pure value judgement, an alternative which would have undermined the legitimacy of the judiciary and then of the the legal process. The judiciary, stripped of their mask of value neutrality, eagerly grasped at the alternative of empiricism. Justice Harlan's opinion in *Katzenbach v. Morgan*[6] is a good illustration. 'Decisions on questions of equal protection and due process', he said, 'are based not on abstract logic but on empirical foundations' (p. 668).

Contrast this with the British legal culture. There is no written constitution and no Bill of Rights to encourage an acceptance of the legitimacy of judicial policy making. There is no equivalent acceptance among the bar or the judiciary in Britain of empiricism as an acceptable alternative to a theory of judicial decision-making based on the more-or-less mechanical application of 'the law' to 'the facts'. Among academic lawyers a new orthodoxy which threatens that judges arrive at their decisions on the basis purely of value judgements is also unsympathetic to an alternative based upon empiricism.

These differing legal cultures are reflected most clearly in the extent to which the adjudicatory institutions have been adjusted so as to be able to fulfill their new policy-making functions. As we have seen, in the USA it is preeminently the federal courts which are utilized to break down segregation. As with other adjudicatory bodies, the key elements of the courts might be summed up as, first, the settlement of disputes by way of 'an authoritative settlement which is imposed on one (or both) of the parties whatever be his attitude towards it' (Weiler, 1968); secondly, an adversary process; and thirdly, a process which arrives at principled and rational decisions, the results of which can be expressed as a rule or standard which can be applied to decide other similar cases.

The attributes of the adjudicatory process may perhaps make for an adequate (or indeed the best) method for finding out events which have transpired between the parties to a lawsuit – what Horowitz calls 'historical facts' (Horowitz, 1977, p. 45). But they do not necessarily help in the ascertainment of the recurrent patterns of behaviour on which *policy* should be based (Horowitz's 'social facts'). Where an adjudicatory body is given the task of policy making, therefore, the body must either make the policy decision without knowing such 'social facts' and thus on inadequately researched premises, or it must adapt its procedures so as to accommodate its new role. The federal courts have adapted their procedures in a number of ways: reliance on expert witnesses; permitting wide discovery of evidence; widespread use and encouragement of 'class action' suits; permitting the use of *amicus curiae* arguments (that is, arguments by those interested in the outcome but with no legal standing); relaxation of 'standing' requirements; encouragements of arguments which explain the social facts (so-called 'Brandeis briefs'); acceptance of the expertise of specialist government agencies; and lastly, willingness to examine the legislative history of an Act which they are interpreting. It may also be worth mentioning the role of the law clerks in this connection, in communicating up-to-date thinking in the law schools from which they have so recently come to the justices and judges for whom they work.

In Britain, also, substantial changes in the legal process have been made. County courts hearing racial discrimination cases sit with assessors who have special knowledge of race relations. Industrial tribunals, to which employment discrimination cases go, comprise not only a chairman with legal experience but also two 'wingmen' who are to provide industrial relations experience. Another important recent development is the participation of the EOC and CRE as *amicus curiae* in a number of appeals in the superior courts, and it may be possible for other non-governmental groups to appear *amicus curiae* too. So too is it possible that experts will be permitted to present their evidence to tribunals in the written form of briefs, similar to American Brandeis briefs, though this has not·yet been attempted. Most important perhaps is the possession of wide ranging strategic powers of investigation by the CRE and the EOC and their power to issue Codes of Practice which industrial tribunals may come to regard as authoritative.

However the unsympathetic British legal culture which I have described is still reflected in certain attributes of the legal system in which the Acts operate and I suggest that these will restrict the effect of the adaptations to the legal system which I have just mentioned. Four main restrictions appear relevant. Firstly, I am sceptical of the extent to which there will be recognition by the judges of areas where relevant social science methodology or expertise will be useful. While the appintment of wingmen does go some way towards building an industrial relations expertise into the industrial tribunal, few have so far been appointed with any expertise in the complexities of racial or sexual discrimination and attempts to inform members of tribunals of the social context of the legislation by way of training has been resisted. The EOC in particular has been pressing for its involvement in training sessions arguing that it could make:

a useful contribution by arranging for systematic discussions of the provisions of the two Acts with lay members of the tribunals. This view has been strengthened by a number of requests from members of tribunals that the Commission should, in conjunction with the Central Office of Industrial Tribunals (COIT) provide guidance on the intentions of the Sex Discrimination and Equal Pay Acts. (EOC, 1976, p. 5)

However, when asked in 1977 by the EOC 'whether any guidance on training has been given to the members of Tribunals and Courts responsible for interpreting and applying the Act about its meaning and effect,' the Lord Chancellor's office replied that no such guidance had been given:

You will appreciate that the interpretation and application of this, or any other law is a matter for the independent judgment of the Courts, and the Lord Chancellor (like other Ministers) must be careful not to do anything which could be construed as an attempt by the executive to guide or influence the decisions of the judiciary. (EOC, 1976, p. 37).

It is unlikely too that in individual cases, at least where the claimant is not represented by Commission lawyers, representatives of complainants will recognize relevant social science issues. Recent decisions on appeal in the area of discovery of documents and information in the course of race and sex discrimination litigation have demonstrated an ambivalence to the quantitative approach. Where relevant information is available, for example, even where an employer has it in his possession already, applicants may not be able to use it to prove discrimination. Even where information is made available, lawyers may not be able to make full use of it. As Cherns (1979) has observed in assessing the conditions for successful interdisciplinary co-operation:

The demands on the social scientist to make himself understood, his advice practical, are familiar. But there is equal need for a corresponding effort on the part of the policy maker to acquire familiarity with the concepts of social science, if only to provide a conceptual framework which enables him to relate 'values' to probable actions. (p. 150)

This condition does not seem to me to be sufficiently fulfilled at present in Britain for social science involvement to be other than minimal.

It would also appear that not only is there little incentive for the complainant to introduce social science evidence, for example by calling expert witnesses, but there is arguably a *disincentive* for him to do so. In purely financial terms, an individual making an indirect discrimination claim (to take the example which probably most involves the potential for social science evidence) may well be worse off financially by calling expert witnesses since even if the plaintiff is successful he can get no damages if the discrimination is proved not to have been intentional. In addition, the system of costs in industrial tribunals, whereby each side bears his own costs no matter what the result, will urge the complainant to greater caution in the use of expensive social science methodology and expert testimony.

There are further restrictions on social scientists participating in a worthwhile manner. Expert witnesses, for example, face the dual problem that while their professional standards call for painstaking and possibly lengthy analysis of an issue, the legal process requires relative immediacy. While professionalism calls for the expert not to be more dogmatic than the data will support, the best witness in a legal confrontation may be one who is decisive, and convincing in his certainty. This is in addition to the unpleasantness of appearing as a witness generally and the low rates of remuneration. 'Why on earth,' as Cantley J. asked in a High Court case, 'should anyone want to be a witness?' (*Daily Telegraph*, 1968).

These restrictions are all, in part, attempts to safeguard the form and primary functions of the courts and industrial tribunals. How can the tension be resolved between, on the one hand, safeguarding the form and primary functions of the tribunals and on the other providing sufficient 'social fact' information to the tribunal on which to base policy decisions?

The current attitude of the Employment Appeal Tribunal (EAT) and the superior courts is by no means consistent on this issue and in different cases different approaches have been taken. On the one hand the EAT in the indirect discrimination *Price*[7] case specifically requested that adequate statistical analysis be carried out at a rehearing in an industrial tribunal. On the other hand, recent equal pay cases indicate that the answer which the courts will eventually give may be that it is not possible to resolve the tension and that informality, speed and lack of expense are more important. Thus in *Fletcher v. Clay Cross (Quarry Services) Ltd.*,[8] the Court of Appeal stressed the need to get away from 'legalism' in the interpretation of the Equal Pay Act and reiterated its desire to return to as uncomplicated a construction of the Act as possible because of the function of industrial tribunals. In that case the Court deliberately so construed the Act as not to require complicated statistical evidence and contrasted its chosen approach with that of a USA case dealing with a similar equal pay issue: 'There will be no need, thankfully, for the kind of statistical evidence covering a period of 28 months, supported by four complicated graphs' used in the US case.[9]

A related issue, and one creating a similar tension, is the vexed issue of representation *by lawyers* of applicants in industrial tribunals. On the one hand informality is the preferred method. On the other, the concept of indirect discrimination, and even more its application, is complex and may well involve intricate legal questions. Again, while the form and primary function of industrial tribunals urge a non-legalistic, broad base approach and a discouragement of further legal participation, the issue of indirect discrimination may require greater involvement of lawyers, at least in the early stages of the development of the Acts. Without expert representation it is even less likely that relevant social science issues will be explored.

Although, as I pointed out above, I would not want to underestimate the potential importance of EOC and CRE use of their strategic powers in introducing and legitimizing the use of social science methodology through taking individual cases to tribunals, conducting formal investigations and issuing Codes of Practice, there seem to me to be two factors which may lessen their impact. One is that in a time of financial stringency, an approach which is unproven in the British context *and* expensive is not likely to be an attractive proposition for funding. Secondly, the industrial tribunals and the courts are ultimately the arbiters of the approach taken. Even after EOC or CRE formal investigations there is a right of appeal from the Commission to a tribunal or a county court.

This judicial review by the superior courts of findings of discrimination by the CRE and EOC may well be a disincentive to the wide ranging use of social science evidence, even in formal investigations, given the inexperience of the courts in dealing with these issues. However, as we have seen, how the courts react to the tension created between their primary functions and these new ones is still uncertain.

Notes

1 163 U.S. 537 (1896).
2 347 U.S. 483 (1954).
3 Separate opinion of Justice Powell in *Keyes v. School District No. 1*, Denver,

Colorado, 413 U.S. 189 (1973).
4   401 U.S. 424 (1971).
5   423 U.S. 820 (1976).
6   384 U.S. 641 (1966).
7   [1977] IRLR 291 (EAT).
8   [1978] IRLR 361 (CA).
9   Per Lawton, L. J., at page 365.

References

Adorno, T. W., Frenkel-Brunswik, E., Levinson, D. J. and Sanford, R. N. (1950), *The Authoritarian Personality*, Harper, New York.

Black, C. Jr. (1959), 'The lawfulness of the segregation decisions', *Yale Law Journal*, **69**, 421.

Brest, P. (1975), *Processes of Constitutional Decison-making,*; Little Brown, Boston.

Cahn, E. (1955), 'Jurisprudence', *New York University Law Review*, 150–169.

Cherns, A. (1979), *Using the Social Sciences*, Routledge and Kegan Paul, London.

CRE (1978), *Commission for Racial Equality Annual Report*, HMSO, London.

CRE (1979), *Commission for Racial Equality Annual Report*, HMSO, London.

Daily Telegraph (1968), 29 November, p. 290. Quoted in Atiyah, P. S. (1970), *Accidents, Compensation and the Law*, Weidenfeld and Nicholson, London, p. 290.

Donovan Commission (1968), *Report of the Royal Commission on Trade Unions and Employers' Associations 1965–1968*, (The Donovan Commission), Cmnd. 3623, HMSO, London.

EEOC (1966), 'EEOC guidelines on employment testing procedures', 24 August, 1966; *EEOC Guidelines on Employment Selection Procedures* (revised) 35 Federal Regulations 12333, 29 Code of Federal Regulations, paragraph 1607, 1 *et seq.*

EOC (1976), *Equal Opportunity Commission First Annual Report*, HMSO, London.

Flanders, A. (1975), *Management and Unions*, 2nd edition, Faber and Faber, London.

HMSO (1980), 'Equal pay and sex discrimination: outcome of applications to industrial tribunals in 1979', *Employment Gazette*, April 1980, 383–386, HMSO, London.

Horowitz, D. (1977), *The Courts and Social Policy*, The Brookings Institution, Washington D.C.

McAuslan, P. (1975), 'The challenge of the environment', in *English Law and Social Policy*, Centre for Studies in Social Policy, London.

Myrdal, G. (1944), *An American Dilemma*, Harper and Bros., New York.

Pound, R. (1912), 'Social problems and the courts', *American Journal of Sociology*, **XVII**, (1912–1913), 334–338.

Pound, R. (1942), *Social Control Through Law*, Yale University Press, New Haven.

Rosen, P. (1972), *The Supreme Court and the Social Sciences*, University of Illinois Press, Illinois.

Sumner, W. G. (1907), *Folkways*, Ginn and Co., The Athanaeum Press, Boston.

Vann Woodward, C. (1966), *The Strange Career of Jim Crow*, 2nd revised edition, Oxford University Press, Oxford.

Weiler, P. (1968), 'Two models of judicial decision-making', *Canadian Bar Review*, **46**, 406–471.

Wolf, E. P. (1972), 'Civil rights and social science data', *Race*, **XIV**, 2.

Research as Evidence and the Proof of Unlawful Racial Discrimination

M. A. PEARN*

Discrimination on grounds of race or sex is a relatively new concept in British law. The first antidiscrimination law made discrimination on grounds of race in public places unlawful (Race Relations Act, 1965) and since then two further Race Relations Acts (1968, 1976) have widened the scope of the law and increased the enforcement powers. In addition, the definition of 'discrimination' has been extended to include not only direct or deliberate discrimination but also the unjustifiable discriminatory effects of policies or practices (*viz* indirect discrimination). Because this law is so new, both the legal system and the public at large are still adjusting to, and assimilating, the new ideas. On the one hand, there is the process by which the courts and industrial tribunals gradually increase their understanding of the nature of discrimination. They become familiar with the pointers or clues which indicate the probability of discrimination and at the same time develop an increased awareness of the purpose and intentions of Parliament. On the other hand, individuals pass slowly through a process of legal socialization whereby they become increasingly acquainted with the nature of discrimination, the objective of equal opportunity and the practical implications for themselves, and their rights (with increased readiness to assert those rights) under the law.

Most cases of discrimination are in the field of employment, and employers also undergo a process whereby they become aware of the existence of the legislation, and gradually evolve an awareness of its implications for them as employers. In terms of understanding the full meaning and implications of the law, all three (*viz* legal system, employers, individuals) are in their infancy. There have still been very few cases where the meaning of the law has developed, very few individual cases are brought, and most managers in

---

*Deputy Director, The Runnymede Trust, London,

industry do not feel threatened by the law. This is partly because the law has had little impact on employers, but also because discrimination is invariably believed to be something perpetrated by others. When managers in industry are asked whether or not they feel they discriminate, either directly or indirectly, the general response can be summed up as: 'no problems here' (Carby and Thakur, 1977).

There is widespread belief that equal opportunity has always been an essential ingredient in employment policies and practices. The only difference is that there is now a new label to put on it, viz. 'equal opportunity'. Consequently, it is sufficient in most cases to formulate a policy to that effect, or a statement, and take no further action (Pearn, 1978). Equality of opportunity is presumed without question; lack of equality of opportunity is the very rare exception. Thus it does not make sense to an employer when claims are made that discrimination is pervasive and that he cannot know whether or not discrimination is occurring without actually investigating the possibility. It does not make sense to hear that active intervention is necessary to detect and prevent unlawful discrimination. How can intervention be necessary when the chances are that it is almost certainly not occurring?

It is perhaps worth reminding ourselves that the notion of equality of opportunity and the definitions of discrimination which are embodied in the law are relatively new and that these ideas will not be fully understood and assimilated quickly. It is unrealistic to expect major changes, associated with major shifts in attitudes and thinking, to occur overnight, or even in the short term, purely as a result of the existence of the Race Relations Act. It is useful to look back to debates on conditions at work 50 years or so ago and to compare them with the state of affairs now. An extract from the Factory Inspectors' Reports 1912–1914 illustrates how far we have come. The following comments concern the working conditions of the fish curers at Yarmouth and Lowestoft:

At the early part of the season it was found that, although the women commenced at 6 a.m., corporation sanitary conveniences were not open until 8.30 a.m. . . . in some of the corporation yards the nearest sanitary convenience for women was about half to three-quarters of a mile away (McCleod, 1978, p. 2).

There are many horror stories of that period which, though they may not necessarily have been typical, indicate by their existence in the absence of any public outcry the degree of change both in terms of the attitudes of employers and the expectations of employees.

The existence of the legislation in itself does create some awareness of the problem of discrimination. This tends to focus attention on blatant and obvious forms (such as discriminatory advertisements) and there is ample evidence that the law has put an end to almost all overt discrimination. Most employers are conscious of the need to prevent and eliminate blatant acts of discrimination. This is regardless of whether or not they recognize that most direct discrimination is covert and indirect discrimination is by its very nature difficult to detect.

In addition, the notion of equality of opportunity is in the air, and is beginning to take its grasp on society. As Glazer (1978) argued in his book on affirmative action, the notion of fairness and equality once developed is very hard to shake off. There are other signs of a changing awareness. Papers on equal opportunity are beginning to appear at management and trade union conferences; the TUC and CBI have issued statements on equal opportunity; and many employers and unions have stated their commitment to equal opportunity. The cynic might well argue that in the absence of appropriate action this is mere window dressing. On the other hand it can be argued that these steps are a necessary (though not sufficient) condition of real progress.

The law on racial discrimination differs from the law on working conditions or health and safety at work or unfair dismissal. Although a period of time must elapse for the new ideas to become familiar and the values internalized, anti-discrimination law may take longer because it is more controversial. It is controversial for a number of reasons and the reasons are part of the cultural climate in which the laws will be interpreted. Whereas few people would say that it is unfair to ask an employer to take steps to prevent the occurrence of accidents or injuries to his employees, they are not so ready to accept that employers should take similar action to prevent the occurrence of unlawful discrimination. Part of the problem is that the racial groups whom the legislators sought to protect from unfair discrimination (*viz* the black population) are a small minority representing little more than 2,000,000 people. They are also a controversial minority because of the political debates about immigration control, repatriation, the fairness of the immigration laws; and the periodic and heated debates on the need to save the country from being 'swamped' by black people. The public debate makes the ethnic minorities feel vulnerable. The Asian and Caribbean populations are frequently described as immigrant despite the fact that nearly half were born in the British Isles. Many people are ready on the one hand to say that discrimination on grounds of race or colour is a bad thing, but on the other argue in favour of restricting access to this country of black people but not white people. Ethnic minority groups are politically sensitive. The existence of extreme right wing organizations such as the National Front constantly bringing the issue into the headlines, and the poor state of relations between police and the young black community are other factors which combine to make black people a sensitive subgroup of the general population. In addition, a proportion of the majority white population can be described as prejudiced and the potential for conflict between black and whites in certain circumstances can be very great. Another aspect is the occurrence of civil disturbance and racial violence, although not on the same scale as that in America, which partially triggered the vigorous enforcement of the Civil Rights Act.

What emerges in Britain is a complex and emotive picture. A cherished ideal of fair play and the honourable treatment of people (which in this context means not discriminating and providing genuine equality of opportunity) interacts with alleged fears about the contry being 'swamped' by black people, conflicts between sections of the black population and the authorities, myths about immigrants, and questions about apparent 'privileges' in law, coupled with moves to alleviate problems of people who, some argue, should not be here anyway.

The emergent picture portrays cherished ideals, uncomfortably juxtaposed to prejudice against black people and controversy over immigration. It is in this context that courts and tribunals will make decisions about particular cases. Can there be a role for psychology here? Tapp (1977) has argued that the role of psychology in the field of law and psychology involves the recognition of its own brands of empiricism and research plus a systematic generating of questions, mapping of data and translating of legal notions. Perhaps the best starting point is consideration of the kind of psychology that is most suited to the interface of psychology and law. As an occupational psychologist, I am interested in the solution of problems which are generated outside the discipline of psychology. One way of doing this would be to equip myself with empirical techniques and conceptual models and to go out in search of problems which will fit the techniques and models. This characterizes much of what we call applied psychology. There is however a distinction to be made between the applied and the applicable (Belbin, 1979). Essentially, applicable psychology focuses on the solution of problems which are generated by people outside the discipline of psychology and the psychological methods employed are regarded as means and not ends in their own right. A great deal of applied psychology is developed as a result of the theoretical interest of psychologists seeking new areas in which both theories and techniques can be tried out. The applicable approach takes the problem as the central focus and may sacrifice some degree of technical sophistication or rigour in the interest of attaining realism, relevence and ultimately the credibility of the findings. Consequently it is often developmental and responsive to factors beyond the requirements of internal validity (for example, experimental design).

The applied psychologist is seeking to contribute more to specialist knowledge than to the solution of real problems. As a result of repeated controlled experiments applying standard methods to a particular kind of subject, he or she may know what works and why it works in a particular setting. The generalization of the findings is severely restricted. Hence the findings may be the result of applied research but in practice they may not be applicable. Another problem associated with applied research is that data generated may not be in a form which can readily be accepted by a different discipline with its different sets of values. For example, it may be relatively easy to simulate aspects of legal or other forms of decision-making in a laboratory task and to produce what may appear to be intriguing results. It would be much harder to apply the results in a meaningful way to the actual real life activity of which the laboratory task was an analogue.

The applicable approach entails a broad understanding of the subject matter under study and flexible attitudes to techniques of investigation which are robust rather than refined, and which will generate useable results. The ultimate test should be the generalizability and applicability of the results. If the results are in any way restricted by being unduly situation-specific, task-specific or are influenced by the very nature of the act of measurement, or based on an inappropriate sample, then the results will not have what Brunswik long ago called, 'ecological validity' (Brunswik, 1955). To be useful in the area of discrimination law, psychological research should achieve a balance between an acceptably high degree of internal validity and maximization of the generalizability of results, coupled with acceptability to the potential users of the research. For the purposes of this paper, the users of the research are lawyers and others who present and adjudicate discrimination cases.

Clearly, the distinction between applied and applicable psychology is one of emphasis and orientation. In reality, the two approaches are opposite poles of a continuum. One feature of the applicable psychologist is that he is able to use terminology which is both meaningful and acceptable to the environment in which he or she is working. This may in part be due to the fact that the terminology and concepts are drawn from that environment rather than from psychology itself. Wherever possible, congruent constructs should be used. In other words, notions, concepts and ideas are used which, as far as possible, are compatible with the same or similar notions in the legal system. An example of a construct lacking conguency, but sharing the same name in psychology and in law, is 'evidence'. Generally speaking, both law and psychology are evidence minded and value conscious but in different ways. It is the task of the psychologist to ensure that the kind of evidence presented and the way it is dependent upon certain values is compatible with the system under study.

It may be useful in this context to examine briefly the impact of applied psychological data on judicial decision-making in the USA, where, with some notable exceptions, there is an almost total dismissal of empirical psychological data by the courts. There seems little doubt that the US Supreme Court decision in *Brown v. Board of Education* in 1954[1] (which put an end to racial segregation in schools) represents the most dramatic use of social science research. The Supreme Court referred to the studies by Kenneth Clark concerning the effects of segregation on black children. It appeared, after this decision, that psychological findings could play a significant role in contributing to the judicial decision-making process by providing relevant empirical data. Unfortunately, the optimism generated at the time does not seem to have been sustained. Although psychologists are often used as expert witnesses providing clarification of certain notions, or providing expert opinion, there is in fact little use of empirical data. Bersoft and Prasse (1978) have reviewed the influence of empirical psychological data on the Supreme Court's decisions on the constitutionality of corporal punishment in schools. They point out that the arguments in favour of abolition and in favour of retention are based on a common research base, and that the same data are being interpreted to support opposite sides of the argument. One of the problems for the courts has been that 'punishment' has a special meaning for psychologists (especially in laboratory settings using animals). This is quite distinct from the general public's idea of punishment, and it is not surprising that the courts are reluctant to draw inferences from laboratory studies when considering punishment in schools.

In his paper, Christoper McCrudden argues that empirical evidence from the social sciences has had very little impact on legal decision-making in the USA. He goes on the argue that he does not think that this kinds of empirical evidence is likely to have much effect on the courts in Britain. I largely agree with this, particularly as it applies to applied psychology, but it may not continue to be true if more research were conducted using the applicable approach. The question is one of providing acceptable and relevant data on the issues where judges themselves see the need for it. Abstract empiricism should be avoided and research should be conducted which is directly relevant to the legal issues (c.f. Skolnick, 1975).

An existing piece of empirical research that could be utilized in this country is the PEP data on the incidence of discrimination (McIntosh and Smith, 1974). The data were obtained from a series of field tests in which matched pairs of candidates applied for real jobs. The candidates were matched in all relevant respects. The difference between members of a pair was either skin colour (black or brown/white) or place of birth (British or foreign born). The incidence of discrimination in selection on grounds of colour was very high. A black person's chances of being discriminated against were:

1 in 2 (unskilled manual)
1 in 5 (skilled manual)
1 in 3 (clerical, administrative).

Direct discrimination is not therefore a rare phenomenon.

It is surprising that this evidence has not been more frequently quoted in tribunal discrimination cases. Perhaps part of the problem is that the field studies involved deceiving the employer (as the applicants were not genuine), and that empirical evidence, however reliable, however convincing, is not going to be acceptable if it is based on deception. This is a great pity because if the PEP findings were widely known and accepted they would undermine the almost unshakable presumption of nondiscrimination by the tribunals. Clearly, if the probability of a black person being discriminated against in the first stage of application for manual, unskilled work is one in two for each job application, then the total number of instances of this kind of discrimination must run into thousands. This number is greatly augmented when other job levels are added. Despite this, only a small number of cases come before a tribunal and of those that do, the success rate is very small (about 10 per cent) (MacDonald, 1979).

Another difficulty with the PEP finding is that it could be criticized in that it does not sufficiently sample different kinds of jobs in different parts of the country, so that average levels of discrimination cannot readily be inferred.

The hardest burden of proof for the individual bringing a case to a tribunal is that discrimination has occurred at all. Direct evidence of discrimination is virtually impossible to produce. The individual applicant is not even in the same position as someone who is challenging an employer on the grounds of unfair dismissal. In this case it is very clear to the individual that he has been dismissed and the burden of proof lies with the employer. In cases of descrimination brought by an individual before a tribunal, the problem is more difficult. The individual feels that he or she may have been discriminated against but the employer need not agree. Therefore the individual has to prove that he/she has been discriminated against. Most of the information will lie with the employer and, in fact, as the records show, it is very difficult to prove discrimination. The few cases which succeed are invariably cases where the discrimination has been either blatant or the employer has made a mistake (for example, saying, 'Oh you're one of those, the lads won't like that'), where the inference of racial discrimination is very difficult to avoid (IDS, 1979). Despite the evidence provided by the PEP studies, the individual has to prove his or her case against an overwhelming presumption of no discrimination.

There are two ways in which empirical evidence collected by psychologists could have a direct influence on courts and tribunals. The first is to assist the proof of a particular case of discrimination, whether direct or indirect. The second is to provide general background information which might enhance the decision-making process of tribunals and courts. As noted above, direct evidence of discrimination is very difficult to produce. Comparative evidence of some kind is probably crucial. If empirical data could show, for example, that differences in treatment between similarly situated persons is highly correlated with the ethnic origin of the persons involved, then in the absence of any adequate nonracial explanation, it would be reasonable to infer that race was the factor causing the difference of treatment. Empirical research on the incidence of discrimination and the factors correlating with it could enhance the tribunal members' understanding of the complex nature of discrimination and provide a framework within which individual cases could be judged.

Statistical evidence of inconsistencies between articulated general statements and what actually occurs in practice would also be relevant to discrimination cases. For example, it is commonly alleged that certain things happen and, in the absence of any evidence to the contrary, it is assumed that they do. Empirical evidence could be produced which showed that under given circumstances, acceptably close to those under consideration, it is rare for those things to happen unless there is direct evidence of their occurrence. As the decision of a tribunal is an inference based on a balance of probabilities rather than conclusive evidence, it does not seem unreasonable that probabilistic statements from empirical data should not enter into the decision-making process in a formal way.

Another form for empirical psychological research which could have application is the hypothesis-testing investigation, which might arise from a formal investigation being conducted by the Commission for Racial Equality. If the Commission believed that word-of-mouth recruiting by an all white labour force would have indirect discriminatory effects because the black members of the labour pool would not get to hear about job vacancies, then this hypothesis could easily be put to the test by an empirical survey. An employer might claim that it does not have women at high levels in the organization because women do not have the necessary skills, personal characteristics, potential or even the interest to become managers. It would not be a difficult exercise to bring in an independent expert to assess their management potential according to agreed terms, and to give an independent third party view – particularly if this could be set in the context of research which showed that it is not uncommon for employers to believe that there is a lack of management potential in female employees, when in fact the potential is there. Another study could result from challenging the claim by an employer that the reason why it does not have ethnic minority employees in supervisory/management positions is that they do not want the jobs. Here a specific enquiry could focus on finding out from ethnic minority employees whether or not they do in fact apply for jobs and if not, the reasons why they do not apply. This research would have little impact on a tribunal unless it could be set in the context of wider research on aspirations. Empirical evidence that job aspirations are correlated with the perceived likelihood of being promoted (that is, being successful in a given context) would also be very relevant.

In the USA, statistics have been used extensively in the proof of disproportionate impact (Schlei and Grossman, 1976). This frequently involves comparing the rejection rates of white job applicants with that of black job applicants, or comparing the numbers of black people employed with the numbers available in the labour market. This is an issue which will be increasingly faced in this country, where the statutory definition of indirect discrimination requires that the complainant prove that a condition or requirement was applied which is considerably harder for the complainant to comply with, and that the failure to do so was to his or her detriment, by virtue of his or her race or sex. Disproportionate or adverse impact has to be proved and already we have experience of a small number of cases involving statistical evidence, but we have not yet faced the methodological problems concerning sample size, comparability of data and the kinds of generalization that can be made.[2]

Another avenue for research would be the investigation of the discriminatory effects (on either individuals or groups) of certain practices or policies. In this respect, the case of *Singh v. Rowntree Mackintosh* (1979)[3] is an interesting one. In this case a no-beards rule in one of seven factories owned by Rowntree Mackintosh disproportionately precluded Sikhs from applying for jobs in the factory. The defence argument was a justification of the requirement based on the assumed gain to health and hygiene by the no-beards rule, even though there might have been an equal gain by a rule permitting beards subject to them being covered by snoods. In this case, it would have been useful to know how many Sikhs would in fact have been prevented from obtaining jobs because of this rule. It would then have been possible to weigh up in more concrete terms the benefits (gains in terms of increased hygiene) and the costs (denial of job opportunity to Sikhs).

A final area of empirical research could focus on the process of decision-making on issues of discrimination. It could be argued that legal decision-making concerning discrimination against ethnic minorities may be different from many other types of decision-making in the courts and tribunals. It was noted earlier that the public debate on race relations and immigration in Britain is controversial. There is a great deal of research data available which suggests that decision-making in general is influenced by factors such as context and the climate of opinion, and the web of assumptions, values and beliefs (of a group or an individual), many of which may now be fully articulated. There is no reason to suppose that industrial tribunal decisions (which are inferences based on the balance of probabilities) should be an exception to the general rule. It would be very interesting to investigate the extent to which decision-making in tribunals reflects not only the attitudes and value systems of tribunal members but also the socio-political climate in which they operate.

A recent decision before an Employment Appeal Tribunal (EAT) can serve as an illustration that tribunal decisions are not exempt from the inconsistencies and irrationalities which characterize much of normal day-to-day decision-making. In this case (*Jalota v. Imperial Metal Industry (Kynoch) Ltd.*, 1979)[4] Jalota had requested the discovery of certain information and documents which he believed were necessary to support his allegation of discrimination against him when he applied for promotion. The response of EAT was that his request was 'wholly unreasonable, irrelevant, and should not be answered'. Jalota had requested statistics on the number of coloured workers employed at a specific grade which he felt would help him show that the employer had a policy of discriminating. He also sought disclosure of confidential information on the educatonal qualifications, age and length of service of the other candidates for the jobs for which he had applied. This was rejected on the grounds that it had been given in confidence. (However, the later House of Lords decision on the *Nasse* case (1980)[5] means that the tribunal Chairman can inspect confidential documents and may order their disclosure if the Chairman considers them necessary to the fair disposal of the proceedings.) Finally Jalota had requested discovery of the undisclosed part of a letter which had been used in the tribunal hearings. The tribunal rejected his request to see the undisclosed part of the letter because Jalota could not show that the section of the letter had any relevance to his case. Jalota was required to prove that the section of the letter was relevant to his case but he was only asking for it to be disclosed in order to know what it contained.

In its commentary on this decision, the Industrial Relations Review and Report stated that EAT had little understanding of the way the law must operate if it is to be even moderately successful, and that EAT had negligible sympathy with the intentions of Parliament. Psychological research on the kind of decision-making illustrated in this case could provide useful material for the training of tribunal members. Macdonald (1979) has noted the tendency of tribunals to draw an inference of no discrimination in a given case where the employers already have black employees. However other tribunals are not prepared to infer the possibility of discrimination from evidence that the employer has no black employees. The nature of inference in industrial tribunal decision-making could be subjected to empirical research. This might well reveal that the decisions are influenced by the personal values of the individuals involved. A survey among managers conducted by the *Harvard Business Review* revealed that solutions given to a set of management problems differed according to whether the key figure in the problem was male or female (Rosen and Jerdee, 1974). It is possible that a similar process could be operating in cases of sex or race discrimination.

A feature of the decisions made by the tribunals in discrimination cases is the small sums of money being offered as compensation for injury to feelings. The sums involved are usually very small, ranging between £25 and £100. Is there a possibility that black people are only offered such small sums by way of compensation because there is an irrational (perhaps unconscious) belief that the very blackness of the complainants in some way caused the discrimination against them and therefore they are in part to blame for it, and the compensation is correspondingly low? It would be of interest to examine decision-making in other contexts and the sums paid out to people because of injury to feeling. There is an increasing research literature on the subject of psychological and physical attraction and the effect of this factor on behaviour and decisions which are otherwise assumed to be rational and sensible.

In summary, there are three broad kinds of psychological empirical research which could have a bearing on the quality of decisions made in cases of racial discrimination. The first is background research, which can be used to create an awareness of the nature and incidence of discrimination and the probability of discrimination occurring under certain circumstances. This broad area would also include study of the effects of discrimination on ethnic minorities both as individuals and as groups. The second kind of research has direct bearing on the actual proof of discrimination, either in general (for example, evidence of disparate treatment, or adverse impact), or in support of a specific case where it may be necessary to use empirical evidence to counter a defence argument or to support a claim (or a hypothesis) by a complainant or the Commission for Racial Equality in the course of a formal investigation. The same techniques could be used by the defence. A third area of research would focus on the process of decision-making in the tribunals, and the way in which inferences are drawn. This research could have implications for the training of tribunal members. Alternatively it could be taken into account by those presenting cases. Perhaps, and this is a remote possibility, it could be used to support an argument for a change in procedures. Ultimately the use that can be made of the research will depend on the exact nature of the findings.

A major problem is of course the acceptability of empirical evidence to the courts and tribunals and the legal system generally. Most traditional applied psychological research is unlikely to be acceptable to the courts and therefore it is not likely to have any influence on legal decision-making. However, the applicable approach may have more potential, especially if it is a response to problems generated within the legal system. If it starts from the need to present to courts and tribunals the kind of evidence which will be acceptable to them in the way it is presented, conceived in the terms of its methodology, and directly relevant to the issues before them, then there is potential for growth in the use of empirical psychological research data. Consequently the psychologist who conducts this research should be familiar with the law and legal processes and should be conversant with the language of law and the conceptual thinking of law. The language and the techniques of psychological research and investigation should be adapted to meet that need. If and only if this approach is developed is there a chance that psychological research evidence will be used by the courts and the legal system generally.

Notes

1   347 U.S. 483 (1954).
2   For a general discussion of indirect discrimination, see Bindman, G. and Grosz, S. (1979), 'Indirect discrimination and the Race Relations Act', in *A Review of the Race Relations Act 1976*, The Runnymede Trust.
3   Industrial Relations Law Reports 199.
4   Industrial Relations Law Reports 313.
5   *Nasse v. Science Research Council*, Industrial Relations Law Reports 465.

References

Belbin, E. (1979), 'Applicable psychology and some national problems: a synopsis of the 1978 Myers Lecture', *Bulletin of the British Psychological Society*, **32**, 241–244.

Bersoff, D. N. and Prasse, D. (1978), 'Applied psychology and judicial decision-making: corporal punishment as a case in point', *Professional Psychology*, **9**, 3, 400–411.

Brunswik, E. (1955), 'Representative design and probabalistic theory in a functional psychology', *Psychological Review*, **62**, 193–217.

Carby, K. and Thakur, M. (1977), *No Problems Here?*, Institute of Personnel Management, London.

Glazer, N. (1978), *Affirmative Discrimination*, Basic Books, New York.

Incomes Data Services (IDS) (1979), 'Race discrimination on the job', *Brief Supplement*, No. 23.

Macdonald, I. (1979), 'Individual enforcement of the Race Relations Act', in *A Review of the Race Relations Act 1976*, The Runnymede Trust, London.

McCleod, E. (1978), *Sixty Years of Achievement*, The Industrial Society.

McIntosh, N. and Smith, D. J. (1974), 'The extent of racial discrimination', *Political and Economic Planning*, **XL**, Broadsheet No. 547.

Pearn, M. A. (1978), *Beyond Tokenism: Runnymede Trust Briefing Paper*, The Runnymede Trust, London.

Rosen, B. and Jerdee, T. H. (1974), 'Sex stereo-typing in the executive suite', *Harvard Business Review*, March–April, Boston.

Schlei, B. L. and Grossman, P. (1976), *Employment Discrimination Law*, Bureau of National Affairs, Washington D.C.

Skolnick, A. (1975), 'The limits of childhood: conceptions of child development and social context', *Law and Contemporary Problems*, **39**, 38–77.

Tapp, J. (1977), 'Psychology and law: a look at the interface', in Sales, B. D., (ed.), *Psychology in the Legal Process*, Spectrum, New York.

Psychological Consequences of being the Victim of a Crime

L. R. C. HAWARD*

After almost half a century of what some people regard as undue concern for the criminal, interest in the victim is now developing, and has already labelled itself as the new scientific discipline of victimology (Drapkin and Vianro, 1975; Teutsch and Teutsch, 1975; Gulotta, 1976). Within its boundaries, three different foci of research have become apparent. The first of these concerns the psychological effects of sexual assault, both in adults and children. This was the first area of victimology studied by psychologists and since Bender's first report (Bender and Blau, 1937) there has been a steady flow of papers in the scientific and medical press on the subject. A second focus of research has been the effects of physical harm from assault and the question of compensation (Miers, 1978), interest in this area leading to the introduction of criminal injuries compensation from Treasury funds. Thirdly, there has been increasing interest in attitudes towards criminals, crime and law enforcement (Ennis, 1967; Fishman, 1979), and particularly in the way attitudes to these aspects of social civilized life are altered by the experience of being a victim of an offence. As Waller and Okihiro (1978) indicate in their extensive study of burglary, the changes in attitude produced by the crime may be more harmful to society than the existence of the crime itself, and this has led them to recommend the decriminalization of certain crimes in the public interest.

Apart from these major issues being examined within the field of victimology, a variety of other problems are being looked at by those who have suddenly discovered the victim as a relatively unresearched subject (Parker, 1979; Marek, Widacki and Hanausek, 1974). One topic which has not yet been studied adequately is the effect of nonsexual crime upon the mental health of the individual. Much of the previous research in victimology is obviously relevant to an examination of questions raised by other studies. Are the

---

*Department of Psychology, University of Surrey, Guildford, Surrey.

long-term psychological effects noted in rape, and in the indecent assault of children due primarily to the physical assault itself, or to the peculiar aspect of the sexual connotation? If the victim suffers mentally as well as physically, to what extent, if any, should such mental trauma be compensated? Does crime-induced psychopathology effect changes in attitudes more than, or differently from, an experience devoid of harmful emotional effects?

Questions such as these occurred to the writer when, in his clinical work, he was asked to examine and treat patients with psychiatric symptoms which had followed closely upon the experience of being victim of a crime. In particular, he was struck by three factors in these cases. First, although such victim-patients represented only a small proportion of a psychiatric caseload, they seemed to come along more frequently than would have been predicted, given the rate of crime in a rural area and the fact that only the more severely disturbed victims would actually reach a specialized psychiatric clinic, most of them being filtered off by the psychiatric registrar, or their family doctor, or their decision not to seek medical help at all. If only the tip of the iceberg was being seen for specialized treatment, then clearly a very substantial number of people were being psychologically disturbed by crimes committed against them. Secondly in discussions with medical colleagues about these cases, it had always been assumed that these patients were already in a latent psychiatric condition, by being significantly neurotic, for example. It was further assumed that the experience of the crime had overwhelmed their low threshold of stress and precipitated the disorder to its present magnitude. However, careful analysis of the psychometric data obtained from these patients showed that as a group the victims seen were no more vulnerable to psychiatric breakdown than any other random sample of the population. This led to the conclusion that the adverse psychological effects of the crime seemed to be more severe than was generally supposed. The third factor observed in this group was that it was not just the assaultive or sexual crimes which preceded a psychiatric reaction: some of the severest reactions came from patients who had not even seen the offender. The psychological response in these cases was clearly to the crime itself, and not to the criminal or to the direct and personal interaction between assailant and victim.

Of course, no general conclusions about reactions to crime can be drawn from a special group of psychiatric patients. As a first step in acquiring a more general data, a preliminary enquiry was set up with the permission of the chief constable and with the full cooperation of the Surrey Constabulary. A special enquiry form was devised and issued to all CID officers investigating crimes, which provides, on one side, questions about the occurrence to be filled in by the police officer, and on the reverse a more detailed questionnaire which the victim was asked to complete as part of the police investigation. The question-naire incorporated clinical items from scales already well standardized on the appropriate population. Returns from the noncorporate victims of the first 120 consecutive crimes reported to one divisional headquarters were obtained. Only one respondent refused to cooperate in the enquiry. The contents of the forms were subjected to statistical analysis, the purpose of this preliminary study being to assess the feasibility of collecting data on psychological reac-tions to crime on a suitable scale and an unselected but geographically circumscribed total victim population. Since this was purely a pilot study it would be inappropriate to use the data as the basis for any firm conclusions, but it may be of interest to look at some of the initial data:

(1) *Sex distribution.* Of the 119 victims cooperating in the enquiry, the ratio was 11 males to 9 females.

(2) *Age distribution.* The age range for such a small sample was unusually large, being from 4 years (a female child assaulted by the grandfather) to 96 years (a man whose house was burgled). The mean age was 36 years but the distribution was bimodal with peaks at 20 years and 50 years. No sex differences were found in the age distribution.

(3) *Type of crime.* The crimes were dichotomized into two categories: one contained the personal direct assaultive crimes, such as common assault, battery (including actual and grievous bodily harm) and rape; the other was concerned with the impersonal indirect crimes, such as burglary, malicious damage, fraud and so on. Forty-four per cent of the sample were victims of the former group of crimes and 56 per cent were victims of the latter category who had no personal contact with the criminal. In toto, the latter crimes were even more numerous than these figures suggest, since it will be remembered that corporate victims were not included in this survey, so that many thefts from retail stores and other business premises were omitted from these figures. In the group of assulted victims 60 per cent were males, and in the group of non-assaulted victims 61 per cent were males.

(4) *Distress.* 117 victims, that is, all but two of the total sample, reported being distressed by the experience of victimization. The two exceptions con-sisted of one man and one woman, both of whom had been assaulted. In addition, some 27 per cent described their distress as bearable and manage-able, and although in many cases they would have benefitted from the help given by a victim support group had one existed in the area, quite clearly these victims did not require professional intervention at a clinical level. In more than two-thirds of the cases, however, clinical support would have been justified, although not all of the victims would necessarily have asked for it or

even accepted it if offered. Forty-two per cent of the whole sample described themselves as *very distressed*, and 92 per cent labelled themselves as being *extremely distressed*. Hence, on a purely symptomatic level, it would be true to say that over 70 per cent of the victims were *substantially distressed*. There were no significant differences between the proportions of each sex in any of the rated grades of distress, men reporting to be just as distressed as the women. By the time of the interview which was carried out within 24 hours of the crime occurring, 25 per cent had got over the distress, while 75 per cent said they were *still distressed*. Two-thirds of the total number of victims thought they would eventually get over their distress, but 27 per cent believed they would be upset for a very long time, and 11 per cent said quite unequivocally that they would *never get over it*. Again, there were no sex differences in the estimation of duration of distress. Various descriptions were obtained of how the victim actually felt as a result of the offence, but these could be crystallized into four general psychological states, most of which were present in all cases, but to differing degrees depending upon the personality of the patient. These states could be crudely labelled as follows: *shock*, which was usually the first response in most cases, and characterized by an inability to cope with the immediate situation; *fear*, which was significantly more prevalent in the assaultive crimes; *anger*, also more prevalent in assault, and *emotional disturbance*, a state which tended to follow the initial reaction and which could be characterized by the presence of psychiatric symptoms, of greater or lesser degree.

Police officers who are officially engaged in dealing with a specific offence, are not the most appropriate people to collect this kind of sensitive psychological material, since they have their primary duties to perform. Moreover, we have no means of knowing how valid are the victim's statements about his reactions, reported retrospectively. We can say his emotional condition as reported at the time of the interview was consistent with the police officers' observations, but no more than this. The accuracy of the predictions of the duration of the emotional reaction could only be evaluated by a suitable follow-up procedure, but the facts that one victim in every 10 said he would never get over the experience is certainly not inconsistent with the experience of the clinical samples of victims, many of whom suffer incidental anxiety conditioning as a result of the offence and which predictably would remain with them forever unless specifically treated.

What can be said on the basis of both clinical experience and the results of this preliminary survey, is that almost everybody is emotionally disturbed by being the victim of an offence; that a large proportion of victims are substantially disturbed; and that a significant number are disturbed to the extent of requiring professional help for what becomes a psychiatric illness. Both men and women are equally vulnerable, and physical contact between criminal and victim is not a prerequisite for serious and chronic psychiatric sequelae. Indeed, the reverse may be true, for while physical injury can soon be forgotten, the awareness that some burgling stranger has contaminated one's initimate and personal chattels can sometimes precipitate intense compulsive-obsessional symptoms which prove highly resistent to treatment and are known to endure for a great many years.

If at this early stage of our studies, we accept that most personal victims of crimes are injured psychologically, sometimes seriously and occasionally permanently, there would seem to be a number of legal implications which deserve comment and possibly discussion. For example, to what extent is the infliction of psychological injury a crime in itself? If not a crime at present, could/should it be conceived as a crime? To what extent is the victim's reaction to the crime a foreseeable consequence of the criminal's conduct? Are there offences of which adverse psychological consequences could *not* be regarded as natural or foreseeable? Is there any practical or theoretical reason, in this respect, to distinguish between the crimes involving personal interaction between criminal and victim, and those where the victim is not conscious of interaction taking place?

A criticism of the present system which is currently being voiced is that on occasions the offender is convicted and sentenced on the basis of a relatively minor offence, when he has actually been instrumental in producing total incapacity of the victim because of the severe psychiatric sequelae consequent to the offence. To what extent the psychological injuries inflicted upon the victim are even made known to the court, much less taken into account, will depend in part upon police discretion, in part upon how well the police keep themselves informed of the victims psychological state, and indeed on the degree to which the victim is willing to communicate to others, psychiatric details which may be embarrassing or even shameful to the victim. Moreover, few victims appear to know their rights regarding compensation for criminal injuries when the latter are not physical.

As human beings develop a more complex and civilized life style, physical damage becomes less likely, and less serious, while pyschological damage becomes more serious and disabling, and man becomes more vulnerable to its effects. During the last half century, the law has developed towards the acceptance of psychological hurt as somewhat equivalent to physical injury – in· divorce actions based on cruelty, for example, but the problems raised in this psycho-legal area are by no means simple, and call for more detailed discussion between lawyers and psychologists.

References

Bender, L. and Blau, A. (1937), 'The reactions of children to sexual relations with adults', *American Journal of Orthopsychiatry*, **7**, 500.

Drapkin, I. and Viano, E. (1975), *Victimology: A New Focus*, Lexington Books (D. C. Heath), Lexington.

Ennis, P. H. (1967), 'Crime victims and the police', *Transactions*, **4**, 36–44.

Fishman, G. (1979), 'Patterns of victimisation and notification', *British Journal of Criminology*, **19**, 146–157.

Gulotta, G. (1976), 'Offender victim system', in Viano, E. C. (ed.), *Victims and Society*, Visage Press, Washington D.C.

Marek, Z., Widacki, J. and Hanausek, T. (1974), 'Alcohol as a victimogenic factor of robberies', *Forensic Science*, **4**, 2, 119.

Miers, D. (1978), *Responses to Victimization*, Professional Books, Abingdon.

Parker, E. (1979), 'Victims of mentally disordered female offenders', *British Journal of Psychiatry*, **124**, 51–59.

Teutsch, J. M. and Teutsch, C. K. (1975), 'Victimology: an effect of consciousness, interpersonal dynamics and human physics', *International Journal of Criminology and Penology*, **3**, 249.

Waller, I. and Okihiro, N. (1978), *Burglary: The Victim and the Public*, Toronto University Press.

Victims of Residential Burglary*

MIKE MAGUIRE†

A crime is, at the least, a disturbance, at the worst, a disaster in people's lives. It is natural for people to want something to be done, just as they do when there has been an accident. This is partly out of a desire for practical action to put things back to normal, as far as possible, but partly it is because people want recognition of the offence, appropriate to its seriousness, from recording the details of a petty theft which is unlikely to be cleared up, to a full-scale murder-hunt (or, in the case of an accident or natural catastrophe, a visit by a government minister to the disaster area.). . . . What offends people's instinctive sense of rightness is that the response is insufficient, rather than that it is insufficiently hurtful to the offender.
(Wright, 1977)

Dr Haward has already drawn attention to the paucity of reliable information available about the psychological effects of nonsexual crime upon victims. Apart from his own work and that of Waller and Okihiro (1978) which he mentioned, the only published material specifically devoted to the question seems to be the reports of various Victims Support Schemes. The most systematic of these was the initial working study by the Bristol Victims Support Scheme (1975) which reported that 7 per cent of the 315 victims contacted during its first six months of operation had suffered a 'severe and long-lasting impact, affecting their life-style' and that 'approximately one third of all victims were upset to a degree which called for some help in restoring normal coping ability'.[2] Most other statistical material is in the nature of 'snippets' too imprecise to be of any real value. For example, Durant, Thomas and Willcock (1972) found that two-thirds of respondents who had come into contact with crime had been 'upset' by the incident and Reppetto (1974) reported that 73 per cent of burglary victims expressed 'considerable fear' of a repeat.

In this paper I shall present some of the results and discuss the implications

*A condensed version of this paper was published in the British Journal of Criminology, Vol. 20, No. 3, July 1980, under the title 'The impact of burglary upon victims'.
†Centre for Criminological Research, University of Oxford.

of interviews with 322 victims of residential burglary carried out in the Thames Valley area between 1977 and 1979. The majority of these interviews took place between four and ten weeks after the burglary was reported[3] and the victims were asked to recall the initial impact as well as the effect upon their lives during the intervening period. The interviewees were drawn from three separate police sectors, one containing a medium-sized market town and surrounding villages, one a town of 130,000 inhabitants and one a wealthy commuter area on the outskirts of London. Although representative of victims reporting burglaries in these areas[4] they are not necessarily representative of burglary victims as a whole. For example, the third area mentioned has very few working-class residents, which affects the overall class balance of the sample. To counteract any bias, care was taken in the analysis to control for factors such as class, sex and age.

It may be of interest to look first at the manner in which people discovered that they had been burgled. Seventy-eight per cent had been out when the burglar entered the house, 16 per cent had been asleep in bed and the remainder had been present and awake. Only 13 (4 per cent) came face to face with the intruder, and for the most part such confrontations were brief and nonviolent, the offender either giving himself up or running away.

Of those who either returned home (most commonly in the early evening) or came downstairs to discover that they had been burgled, the majority first noticed not as one might expect drawers turned out and property scattered about the floor, but simply one or two minor changes to the appearance of the house. Open or broken windows were the most frequent first signs seen. Other typical indications were ornaments dropped or knocked over, cupboard doors or drawers opened, or items moved to different places in the room. The word 'ransacking' could be used sensibly in no more than 12 per cent of cases.

About 20 per cent were in the house for some time (several days in a few cases), before they realised that articles were missing, but even among those who immediately knew that something was wrong it often took a period of 10 seconds or more to associate the signs they saw with the word 'burglary'. Their first instinct seems to have been to find a more 'normal' explanation of what had occurred. For example:

No. 37   I saw everything on the floor and I thought my boys had been having a party. I was halfway up the stairs to tell them off before I did a sort of double take.
No. 100   I looked over where the television should be and it wasn't there. It's funny, it didn't click at all, even then. It was only when I noticed the gloves that the truth began to dawn. It was a horrible sinking feeling in my stomach.

One victim likened the feeling to being in a road accident, with an initial refusal to believe what had happened, and a 'sense of unreality', followed about one minute later by 'sheer panic' when the truth became clear.

Initial Impact

All victims were asked to describe in their own words their first reaction once they realised what had happened. The answers were fairly easily classifiable into six categories (see Table 1).

Table 1. What was your first reaction on discovering the burglary?

Reaction	Male	Female	All
Anger/annoyance	41%	19%	30%
Shock	9%	29%	19%
Surprise/disbelief	11%	6%	9%
Upset/tears/confusion	13%	20%	17%
Fear	4%	13%	9%
No strong reaction	21%	13%	17%
Total	100% (N=163)	100% (N=159)	100% (N=322)

The most common reaction was one of anger or annoyance, experienced by 30 per cent of respondents. Shock (19 per cent) and general emotional upset (17 per cent) were also relatively frequent, but only 9 per cent stated that fear had been their first feeling. Seventeen per cent reported feeling calm or unworried. Women were more likely than men to react with shock, fear or upset, while the typical male response was one of anger. There was also a class difference,[5] working-class respondents of both sexes reporting shock, fear and upset more frequently than middle-class interviewees. Of course, all these categories can include anything from mild to very severe reactions. Those who experienced shock ranged from a woman who 'felt the need for a glass of brandy' to one who 'shook and shook for several days'. 'Anger' ranged from indignation to blind fury; and 'upset' from mild depression to hysteria. Precise measurement of the intensity of reactions was extremely difficult, as some victims were inclined to use exaggerated language ('petrified' "flabbergasted" 'fuming', etc.) to describe their feelings while others played them down in retrospect. Our subjective assessment was that at least 20 (6 per cent) of the 322 victims interviewed had suffered serious distress shortly after discovering the crime. Their reactions included acute shock, trembling, panic and uncontrolled weeping. The following are examples of such cases reported in the victim's own words:

No. 536   I went to pieces. I just couldn't believe it. I cried so much I couldn't phone the police. I was so frightened. I cried every time someone talked to me.
No. 825   It was the worst shock of my life. The doctor had to give me an injection. I couldn't speak a word.
No. 1010   I was hysterical. I ran screaming to my neighbour and hammered on her door. Then I went icy cold and shivered for hours.

One woman said she had been found by neighbours 'standing dumbstruck in the middle of the street', and two others reported being physically sick.

The extent of the emotional impact appears to vary considerably between different social groups. Eighteen of the victims aged above 20 were female, 11 were working-class and 8 were pensioners, all these groups being over-represented. It was also interesting that 12 were widowed, separated or divorced, although only 18 per cent of the total sample fell into this category – a point that will be discussed later.

In addition to the 20 suffering serious distress, we identified a further 63 victims (19 per cent of the total) upon whom the initial impact appeared to have been fairly strong. Female victims were again overrepresented among them (although not to such a significant degree), but there was little difference by age or class. Once again, a brief selection of this second category are quoted to give a flavour of the nature of the reactions:

No. 142   I was shaken to the core. The idea of someone in my house – somehow I felt violated.
No. 144   Everything was unreal. I was in a dream. There was just this feeling that someone had been walking about in my house.
No. 650   I was really frightened – I was trembling. I thought they could have come upstairs. It never hits you till it happens to you.
No. 762   It was the most terrible feeling to think tht someone's been in your house. I nearly made myself sick with shaking.
No. 861   I was very shocked at first. It's a feeling that you don't own your own house.
No. 920   When I saw the window I practically heaved up. I didn't know what to do.
No. 1597   I turned to jelly for half an hour. I was very shocked and tearful and had to have a few drinks.
No. 1717   I got the spooks. I went round looking in all the cupboards and under the beds to convince myself they weren't still in the house.
No. 1779   I am used to crime [a barrister] but it was still a bad shock, much worse than I thought it would be. I felt so unsafe.

Lasting Effects

Although at least one-quarter of victims experienced some very unpleasant moments after discoverng that they had been burgled, this alone can hardly be regarded as a serious social problem. What may be of more concern is the lasting impact of burglary.

About 65 per cent of victims interviewed 4–10 weeks after the event said it was still having some effect upon their lives. The most common persisting effects were a general feeling of unease or insecurity and a tendency to keep thinking about the burglary.

Once the initial shock had worn off, most victims began to speculate about who had committed the offence. As less than 30 per cent of burglaries are cleared up by the police, the majority never find the answer to the riddle and the imagination is allowed full rein. While some continue to envisage a frightening stranger (typically employing terms such as 'rough', 'scruffy', or 'unemployed' when asked to describe their mental picture of him) more than half came on reflection to suspect that the burglar was in fact 'somebody local' who knew them or was familiar with their habits.[6] On the whole, the latter conclusion was more likely to prolong the worry caused by the burglary. Victims tended to reinterpret small events in the past – arguments with neighbours, visits to the house, 'nosey' questions, etc. – as related to the burglary. For example, one woman told us that she now 'suspected everybody' of being the culprit. She was convinced that 'he know his way around', having chosen one of the few times she was not in the house to commit the offence and having quickly found some cash she had thought well hidden. She said she was 'racking her brains' as to who could have done it: 'Your have this awful suspicion about everybody who comes near your house: the milkman, the kids, even people you have known for years'.

Such feelings had developed in at least three cases into a state approaching paranoia, where the victims were convinced that somebody – they did not know who – held a grudge against them and was 'watching' them. Even in less serious cases, people were inclined to search for reasons why their house had been chosen among all the possible targets in the area, and this tendency (which we dubbed the 'why me?' syndrome) seems to have been responsible for a great deal of the anxiety produced by burglaries.

Another common consequence of suspecting acquaintances – one which was named by 7 per cent of victims as the worst effect of the burglary – was a general sense of disillusionment with humanity. An example is provided by case No. 29, a 40 year-old man living alone who lost a week's wages from his jacket. He said that prior to the burglary he regularly invited workmates back for meals and social evenings, had people to stay overnight, and so on. He had always trusted people and welcomed them into his house. When he returned one evening to find his back window broken and the money taken he described his initial reaction as intense anger followed by a 'complete loss of faith in people'. As he guessed, the offender was a previous visitor to the house, but even after the latter had been arrested the victim's attitude to others remained radically altered. As he put it, he had changed from an 'open' to a 'closed' person, and was now reluctant to have anybody in his house.

Fifteen per cent of victims stated that they were still frightened at times as a result of the burglary. This normally took the form of fear when entering the house or certain rooms in the house or of being alone in their homes during the hours of darkness. Many of these thought that now the burglar knew the 'layout' of the property he might return to steal what he had not taken originally.[7] The main physical consequences of such fear were difficulty in sleeping (8 per cent mentioned this) and the use of tranquillizers or other drugs not previously taken (3 per cent). In all, 6 per cent said that their physical health had suffered as a result of the incident.

The most striking long-term psychological effect was almost exclusively experienced by women. About 12 per cent of all females interviewed used words such as 'pollution', 'violation', or 'a presence in the house'. Many made an explicit analogy with a sexual assault, expressing extreme revulsion at the idea of a 'dirty' stranger touching their private possessions, and had felt impelled to 'clean the house from top to bottom'. Such effects tended to persist for several weeks and were so disturbing in two cases that the victims had decided to move house to escape them. Five others had burnt furniture or clothing touched by the burglar. The following examples show the intensity of feeling that could be aroused:

No. 539   I shall never forget it because my privacy has been invaded. I have worked hard all my life and had my nose to the grindstone ever since and this happens. Now we can't live in peace. I have a feeling of 'mental rape'. I feel a dislocation and disruption of private concerns. I have destroyed everything they touched, I feel so extreme about it.
No. 629   I'll never get over the thought that a stranger has been in here while we were in bed. . .the idea that a stranger, who could be one of those horrible revolting creatures, has been mauling my things about.
No. 976   They had gone through all my clothes. I felt a real repulsion – everything felt dirty. I wanted to move – I had nightmares, and it still comes back even now.
No. 1010   It's the next worst thing to being bereaved; it's like being raped.

A final common effect upon victims was to change what we called their 'security behaviour'. Of those who had not been insured 43 per cent took out a policy, and 42 per cent of those who had been under-insured increased their cover. Fifty per cent improved the physical security of their homes by fitting new locks or bolts or an alarm. Eighty per cent of those who admitted they had been careless about locking doors or shutting windows prior to the burglary said that they had become more 'security-conscious' as a result (although some were already beginning to 'lapse'). A very small minority went to desperate extremes, nailing up windows, putting furniture against doors, or sleeping with weapons beside the bed. With the possible exception of insurance, most of the above activities seemed to have a greater psychological than practical purpose. Victims generally recognized that it is impossible to create a 'thief-proof' house, but the very act of making it more difficult to get in gave them some sense of control. As one man put it, 'I felt I was fighting back'. Others simply said they 'felt better afterwards'.

In addition to describing their reactions victims were asked what, looking back, had been the worst thing about the whole event. The question was put twice during the interview, on the second occasion asking them to choose one or more possibilities from a prepared list. Table 2 shows the results of this second exercise.

Table 2. What was the worst thing about the burglary?

	Selected as worst	Selected as second worst	Mentioned as either first or second choice
Intrusion on privacy	41%	22%	63%
Emotional upset	19%	25%	44%
Loss of property	25%	20%	45%
Disarrangement of property	4%	4%	3%
Damage to property	3%	2%	5%
None of these	7%	27%	
Total	100% (N=322)	100% (N=322)	

Sixty per cent selected either intrusion on their privacy or general emotional upset as the worst element.[8] This finding underlines the significant point that the emotional impact of burglary is more important to victims than financial loss. While victim research (cf. McDonald, 1976) has paid attention to the possibilities of restitution or compensation, our study suggests that at least where burglary is concerned the emphasis would more appropriately be placed upon the alleviation of psychological effects.

Differential Susceptibility to Longer-term Effects

We have already seen that certain categories of victim such as female, pensioner, separated or divorced), appear to suffer disproportionately heavy initial effects. To test relative susceptibility to longer-term effects we asked a panel of volunteers to assess each case. Ten people from a variety of backgrounds were given a copy of every victim's account of the effects the burglary had had upon his or her life up to the time of interview, and were instructed to rate each one in terms of the overall impact the burglary had produced, using a scale from 1 (severe) to 5 (little or none). The answers were averaged, cases with an average of 1.5 or below being labelled 'serious effects', those with an average between 1.5 and 2.5 'fairly serious' and so on.

The group emerged as follows:

Serious	(1 to 1.5)	43
		(13%)
Fairly serious	(1.5 to 2.5)	71
		(22%)
Moderate	(2.5 to 3.5)	100
		(31%)
Slight or nil	(3.5 to 5)	108
		(34%)
		322
		(100%)

This exercise confirmed that, as with the initial reaction on discovering a burglary, the most serious lasting effects are largely confined to *female victims*. Although almost equal numbers of males and females were interviewed, 34 of the 43 deemed to be worst affected were women. We therefore concentrated most of our analysis upon female respondents only, looking for any significant differences between the characteristics of those women who were badly affected and those who were not.

The most striking finding was that no less than 21 (62 per cent) of the 34 most affected were *separated, widowed or divorced*, although only 49 (31 per cent) of the total female population interviewed fell into this category (see Table 3).

Other victim characteristics we measured had very little independent effect. For example, *female pensioners* were more seriously affected than women under 60, but much of this difference can be explained by the presence of 18 widows among the 35 pensioners.[9] *Working-class women* were marginally worse affected than middle-class women and *women living alone* worse than those living with others, but both these groups contained a higher proportion of widows and divorcees. When the figures were controlled for marital status, the differences all but disappeared. Overall, the category of women emerging as most seriously affected was *working-class widows over 60*, but once one starts subdividing classification, the numbers become too small to allow full confidence in the results (see Table 4).

Table 3. Effects on female victims by marital status

	Married	Single	Separated/ divorced	Widowed	Total
Serious effects	8	5	10	11	34
Less serious effects	67	30	15	13	125
Total	75	35	25	24	159

($x^2 = 19.8$ with 3df $p > 0.001$)

The Bristol Victims Support Scheme research mentioned earlier found that the worst effects of victimization fell upon *females living alone*. Chris Holtom of Bristol University, who directed the survey, kindly lent us the original data, from which we selected out the 135 cases of burglary. It is interesting that 10 of the 12 female victims whom the volunteers considered had suffered 'maximum impact' or were 'very upset' were in fact separated, widowed or divorced. Once again, this was the strongest predictor of serious effects.

Table 4. Selected categories of victims interviewed, showing percentage seriously affected

	Victims seriously affected		No. in sample
Women	34	(21.4%)	159
Working-class women	16	(24.5%)	65
Women living alone	17	(28.3%)	60
Women over 60	12	(34.3%)	35
Divorcees	10	(40.0%)	25
Widows	11	(45.8%)	24
Widows living alone	9	(50.0%)	18
Working-class widows	6	(60.0%)	10
Working-class widows over 60	5	(62.5%)	8
All victims	43	(13.4%)	322

We had expected that, independent of the characteristics of the victim, the *nature of the offence* would make a considerable difference to its impact upon the household – for example, that night-time burglaries would create more fear than daylight offences; offences where the victim was present more than those where the house was unoccupied; 'break-ins' more than 'walk-ins'; and so on. However, none of these factors had any significant effect. Nor, indeed, did the type or value of the property stolen: people who lost nothing at all were as likely to be badly affected as those losing hundreds of pounds. The one exception was in the case of *ransacking*. Eight of the 18 women interviewed whose property had been seriously damaged or disarranged were among the most seriously affected.

Explanations and Implications

There is little doubt on the evidence presented here that a burglary is a significant event in the lives of a considerable proportion of victims. Almost all those we interviewed had a clear memory of their reactions on discovering that their house had been entered. As many as 25 per cent (and 40 per cent of all female victims) were fairly seriously shocked or distressed at the time, and more than a month after the event only one-third of all victims said that they had fully recovered from the experience. Fifteen per cent were still in some fear, about one in eight women felt 'contaminated' or 'violated' and others reported worry, difficulty in sleeping, reluctance to leave the house un-occupied and a distrustful and suspicious attitude to strangers. Above all, the impression was of people struggling to recapture a lost sense of security.

The irony is that the event triggering off such responses was often objec-tively a fairly trivial incident. Most of the victims quoted had lost very little and their houses had not been ransacked; more often than not it was still daylight when they discovered the offence and there was no sign of the offender. Many even suspected local teenagers of whom they would not be physically afraid if confronting them.

Before any remedies for the problem can be suggested, it is essential to attempt to understand why it occurs. There seem to be at least three possible explanations, none of which is fully satisfactory, but which at least provide some illumination in a proportion of cases.

The first is simply that those who react badly are often people who are already of a nervous and insecure disposition, and that *any* unexpected un-pleasant experience might cause a similar reaction. This idea, although not properly testable on our evidence, might be supported by the preponderance of older women, widows and separated and divorced women among those who suffered the worst initial impact. On the other hand, there was also a considerable number of victims to whom the above description clearly did not apply and yet who described strong symptoms of shock. Dr Haward has also made the point in his paper that those he treated for psychiatric conditions following victimization 'were no more vulnerable to psychiatric breakdown than any other random sample of the population'.

The second explanation is concerned with the public image of burglary. As Waller and Okihiro have pointed out (1978, p. 36), media accounts of burglaries tend to sensationalize the offence and exaggerate the dangers, thereby needlessly increasing public fears. One might even criticize crime prevention literature on the same grounds. Even disregarding such influences, one has only to think back to childhood fears of 'noises in the night' to understand why burglary comes high on the list of crimes people fear might happen to them.[10] It thus seems plausible to interpret the initial symptoms of shock so frequently mentioned (shivering, pallor, nausea, etc.) as a result of the combination of the *unexpectedness of the event* and the *imagination of the victim*. As previously described, many victims are temporarily unable to understand what has happened. If this state of disorientation is followed by a moment of comprehension, in which a word with frightening connotations such as 'burglars' suddenly leaps to mind, all sense of prespective can be lost and the victim may react to his or her preconceived image of what burglary entails rather than to the (usually less serious) reality of the situation. Many of those we interviewed recovered from the initial impact within a few hours, which may be a manifestation of the gradual replacement of flights of imagination by a more objective manner of viewing the incident.[11]

A third possibility is that the victim is reacting instinctively to an invasion of his or her private territory. This is supported by the frequent mention of 'violation' and disgust at 'the idea of someone in my house', the latter being chosen as the worst element by many. Psychologists such as Lorenz (1966) have emphasized the importance of feelings towards personal territory. However, although these no doubt play a part in intensifying victim reactions, we found no correlation between the degree of attachment to one's home and the severity of reaction after it has been invaded.[12]

Each of the three explanations seems to imply a different general approach to reducing the adverse effects of burglary. The first points towards awareness of and action to help types of people particularly susceptible to distress. Victim Support Schemes have already found that the aged and people living alone are likely to require more support than most. Our finding that separated, divorced and widowed women are the most vulnerable group may be of help in their allocation of resources, although how to actually locate such people is not an easy task.

The second raises the problematic issue of public attitudes towards and fear of crime. Waller (1970) has brought upon himself a great deal of criticism and misunderstanding in Canada by tackling this boldly. Starting from the assumption (supported by a number of research findings[13]) that fear of crime may often be as socially harmful as actual victimization, he has suggested a programme of 'de-dramaticization' of burglary, involving fewer prosecutions for minor offences, elimination of fear-producing crime prevention campaigns, and efforts to educate the public 'by more frequent publicity of the peaceful nature of residential burglary'. He has also advocated that minor burglaries should be merely recorded over the telephone by civilian employees with an explanation to the public of the scarcity of police resources, so that trained policemen can concentrate upon 'more serious offenders' (Waller and Oki-hiro, 1978, p. 105). These ideas have brought heated responses such as that by McKay (1978):

I would like him [Waller] to be aware that the burglary was neither common nor dull for us. It was in fact an intrusive and psychologically violent act with long-term and enduring consequences. The impact of having our home, privacy and personal belong-ings violated in a distinctly impersonal fashion was, I can assure him, not dull. . . .

If anything, our residual anxiety over the act was heightened by what we perceived as the *lack of reaction* by the local police. Frankly, in the aftermath of such an incident one resents being treated as mundane routine. Contact with the local force reflected less than five minutes of total conversation on the telephone with the investigating officer and with a desk officer at the station.

The third explanation – emphasizing the importance of a home as a secure 'territory' within which people feel safe – raises questions of protection, either through locks and bolts or (more ambitiously) by 'defensible space' policies such as those advocated by Newman (1972). Whether or not such methods are effective in reducing crime does not concern us here. The interesting point is that a high proportion of victims, many of them in the full belief that 'if they want to get in, they'll get in', found it comforting to change their locks or install new security devices. The visit of a crime prevention officer or even a few simple 'tips' by the investigating police seemed equally helpful in reestablish-ing a sense of security, although again victims recognized that their house was by no means thief-proof. A possible conclusion is that victims should be actively advised and encouraged to make some changes, if only minor, in the protection of their homes.

My main purposes have been to present information and to raise questions rather than to argue for a definitive solution to the problems. However, I shall finish by putting forward some suggestions based on my own view of the situation. A key point, perhaps underemphasized by Waller and others, seems to be the difference between *anxiety that a crime might happen* and *anxiety following an actual victimization*. There need not necessarily be a contradiction between encouraging a less 'dramatic' public attitude towards burglary and taking seriously the psychological impact upon those who become victims. While it seems sensible to discourage sensational reports and campaigns which may increase public fear, this approach need not be taken to the extreme of making victims feel apologetic or embarrassed to report offences and to ask for attention. Indeed, McKay's point above, that the *lack* of police reaction heightened his family's anxiety is supported by the results of our interviews. About one third of our sample had some criticisms of the manner in which their case had been handled by the police, by far the most frequent complaint being that the police had displayed a 'lack of interest' or had 'treated us as unimportant'.[14] There was also criticism that once the police had left, no notification was given about the progress (or lack of progress) made in the case. What emerged from questions about what they wanted from the police was that on the whole victims were less concerned with seeing an offender arrested than with receiving what they regarded as the *appropriate response to the incident*. This included showing sympathy and interest, taking fingerprints, questioning neighbours, giving advice on security and later reporting back on progress. As in many cases there is little hope of an arrest,[15] the above actions can often be regarded as virtually a ritual to be performed. Many of those whose cases had been handled with this kind of close attention, although intellectually recognizing that it had had no tangible results in terms of solving the crime, stated that the results had been beneficial in helping them recover their stability.

Others who had come to terms with the burglary fairly quickly said that they had been helped by simply 'talking out' the event with a friend, and it was not uncommon for interviews to end with the victim saying that our visit had fulfilled a similar function. Having completed the interview we sometimes stayed to continue talking, and in the course of discussion mentioned our findings that the majority of arrested burglars are teenagers, that few ever offer violence to householders, and that on average people are victimized only twice in a lifetime, all of which seemed to help people take a more realistic and balanced view of their own burglary. Victim Support Schemes have also found that one or two visits to 'talk over' the burglary are all that is required in the majority of cases to help people over the worst effects.

To conclude, in both the general public fear of crime and the emotional upset caused by victimization the common enemy seems to be people's overactive imagination. It seems logical that anxiety can be reduced on the one hand by the kind of 'educative' programmes recommended by Waller, and on the other by the very opposite of another of his recommendations, that is, by *more* rather than less attention to those who have actually suffered a burglary. The latter could be achieved by changes in police attitudes or by the extension of Victim Support Schemes, or ideally by both. The burden upon police time would not necessarily be greatly increased if a special effort was made to impress upon junior officers the value (in terms of both better police–public relations and of aid to victims) of awareness of the feelings burglary produces and of taking simple steps to deal with them. In most cases all that is required is to encourage those affected to express their fears, pointing out gently that the burglar is probably a harmless teenager who selected the house at random and is unlikely to return, and carrying out the basic ritual of investigation in a reassuring and thorough manner. Ideally, if volunteer Victim Support Schemes could be developed in more areas, the investigating officer could offer to arrange for a visitor to come if the victim needed more help.

Many experienced officers (particularly uniformed) already act in this manner, and a substantial proportion of interviewees paid them compliments for it. However, we were made aware of a strong feeling, especially among working-class victims, that the police 'are not what they used to be' and it seems important to draw attention to this undercurrent.

Ultimately, of course, the question of finances and resources may decide the issue: whether or not public funds can be spared to development support schemes and whether police administrators believe that too much time is already allocated to visits to the scenes of minor crime are factors for argument. Nevertheless, the damage done over the long term by the insecurity and mistrust of others that burglary fosters and by the sense of having been 'short-changed' by a casual or unsympathetic response by the police seems, from the results of our study, to deserve some serious consideration.

Nils Christie has drawn attention to the way in which conflicts between individuals (and burglary can be considered as such) have been 'taken over' by professionals: 'Victims of crime in particular have lost their right to participate' (Christie 1977, p. 1).

The victim of a burglary is surely entitled to at least 'recognition of the offence' and if possible, some 'practical action to put things back to normal' (Wright, 1977, in the opening quotation of this article).

Notes

1   The writer, a Research Officer at the Centre for Criminological Research, recently completed a comprehensive survey of the incidence and effects of burglary in a dwelling in the Thames Valley area, 1975–1979, and intends to publish the result shortly in book form.

2   The scheme sent volunteers to visit all victims of indictable crimes reported in South Bristol excluding those against commercial establishments and thefts of and from cars. Ninety-seven per cent of cases involved thefts or burglaries.

3   The interviews, which lasted on average about one hour, were carried out in the victims' homes by myself and a research assistant, Dr Trevor Bennett, now a Senior Research Officer at the Institute of Criminology, Cambridge.

4   The response rate was 62 per cent and there were no significant differences in terms of class, value stolen, method of entry or untidiness of search between respondents and nonrespondents.

5   'Working-class' was defined as all those household where the main provider of income was employed under Registrar-General's classes III M, IV or V; and 'middle-class' those under I, II and III N. Retired and unemployed were classified according to their previous employment.

6   This was more frequently the case in housing estates or in streets close to housing areas perceived as containing 'problem families'. Residents of Gerrards Cross, a predominantly middle-class town, were much more likely to believe that the culprit was a travelling stranger.

7   In fact, only 11 of the 322 interviewed were burgled again during the period of study. We were aware of the interest by victimologists in the phenomenon of multiple victimization (for example, Sparks, Genn and Dodd, 1977, p. 231) but apart from a case where some children had stolen a neighbour's key, which they used to enter her house several times, we found no evidence of burglars deliberately returning to the same house.

8   Of course, the low numbers who chose damage or disarrangement of property as the worst thing about the burglary were to some extent produced by the comparatively few cases in which there was any serious damage or ransacking. In addition, the 14 per cent who lost no property could not select loss as the worst element. However, even allowing for these factors, victims were still likely to select an emotional element as the worst. Thus, only 16 per cent of those who had to pay over £15 to repair damage selected 'damage' as the worst thing; 14 per cent of those whose property was scattered on the floor selected 'disarrangement' as the worst thing; and 29 per cent of those who lost any property selected 'loss' as the worst. Broadly similar results were obtained from the same question when there was no precoded set of choices, but they provided a little extra insight. It was striking how many victims answered with almost identical words: *'The thought that someone had been in my house'*. Twenty-two per cent used this phrase or a very close equivalent. The answers also showed that many of those most concerned about the loss of their property were upset by *sentimental* rather than financial value.

9   While eight of these 18 widows suffered badly, only four of the remaining 17 older women did so. Male pensioners, too, were almost as resilient as younger male victims.

10   For example, a *New Society* survey (29 September 1966) found that 26 per

cent of a random sample of the population 'worried a great deal' about the possibility of being burgled, while only 16 per cent worried about being physically assaulted.

11 Sparks *et al.* (1977, p. 208) have even suggested that the actual experience of victimization reduces fear of crime by (in most cases!) showing the victim that the reality is not as serious as the imagined event, although this finding is challenged by some Canadian research (Grenier and Manseau, 1979).

12 Although we found two specific categories of people – students in 'digs' and servicemen renting houses while stationed at a base – who were almost all unaffected by their burglaries, the numbers were too small to generalize and anyway special cultural factors may explain this. Moreover, it transpired that owner-occupiers, who might be thought to have more emotional attachment to their property than those who rent, were less seriously affected than both tenants of private landlords and council tenants. Waller and Okihiro (1978, p. 37) also found no relationship between length of residence and severity of reaction, nor did it make any difference whether or not people had put extra effort into major alterations or decoration in their home.

13 For example Furstenberg (1972), Garofalo (1977), Hindeland Gottfredson and Garofalo (1978) Garofalo and Laub (1978). Such studies of the general fear of crime have shown a substantial level of public apprehension and a tendency to overestimate one's chances of becoming a victim.

14 Twenty per cent of working-class victims – who were generally more critical than middle-class victims – made this complaint and 5 per cent were extremely bitter about the way they had been treated.

15 A fact acknowledged by police and victims alike: victims described the police estimation of the chances of arrest as 'optimistic' in only 20 per cent of cases and they themselves were even less hopeful.

References

BVSS (1975), 'Summary of first six months work of Bristol Victims Support Scheme', mimeo, University of Bristol.

Christie, N. (1977), 'Conflicts as property', *British Journal of Criminology*, **17**, 1, 1–15.

Durant, M., Thomas, M. and Willcock, H. D. (1972), *Crime, Criminals and the Law*, Office of Population Censuses and Surveys, HMSO, London.

Furstenberg, F. (1972), *Fear of Crime and its Effects on Citizen Behaviour*, Bureau of Social Science Research, Washington D.C.

Garofalo, J. (1977), *Public Opinion about Crime*, U.S. Department of Justice, Washington.

Garofalo, J. and Laub, J. (1978), 'The fear of crime: broadening our perspective', *Victimology: An International Journal*, **3**, 34, 242–253.

Grenier, H. and Manseau, H. (1979), 'Les petits commerçants victimes de vol à main armée en quête de justice', *Criminologie*, **XII**, 1, 57–65.

Hindelang, M., Gottfredson, M. and Garofalo, J. (1978), *Victims of Personal Crime*, Ballinger, Cambridge, Massachusetts.

Lorenz, K. (1966), *On Aggression*, Methuen, London.

McDonald, W. F. (ed.) (1976), *Criminal Justice and the Victim*, Saga, Beverley Hills.

McKay, B. (1978), Letter in *Liaison*, **4**, 11, 4, in reply to an article 'Minor burglary' by I. Waller.

NACRO (1977), *Guidelines for Developing a Victims Support Scheme*, NACRO, London.

Newman, O. (1972), *Defensible Space*, Macmillan, New York.

Reppetto, T. A. (1974), *Residential Crime*, Ballinger, Cambridge, Massachusetts.

Sparks, R. F., Genn, H. and Dodd, D. (1977), *Surveying Victims*, John Wiley London.

Waller, I. and Okihiro, N. (1978), *Burglary: The Victim and the Public*, Toronto University Press.

Waller, I. (1970), 'Victimisation studies as guides to action: some cautions and suggestions', paper presented to Third International Symposium on Victimology, Muenster, 2–8 September, 1970.

Wright, M. (1977), 'Nobody came: Criminal Justice and the needs of victims', *Howard Journal*, **XVI**, 1, 22–31.

Observations on Dispute Dynamics and Resolution Hearing Outcomes in a Small Claims Court*

NEIL VIDMAR†

Within the past decade considerable interest has focused on alternative procedures for resolving minor legal disputes in North America. The problems encompassed in the interest range from consumer complaints through domestic disputes to minor criminal matters. Various experiments with forums for handling these disputes have ranged from minor modifications in court procedure to independent neighborhood justice centres and the modes of resolution encompass varying forms of mediation/conciliation, arbitration and adjudication.

There are a number of reasons for this interest. On the one hand there is a concern with administrative efficiency; court dockets have become clogged with cases and alternatives are sought to ease the pressure. On the other hand there is the concern that legal procedure does not provide justice for many kinds of problems (for example, it is expensive and time consuming; its flexibility in providing solutions for specific problems is severely constrained; it forces disputants into conflict instead of seeking ameliorative solutions that get at the underlying causes of disputes). It is further argued that because of the above reasons many people who have problems simply endure them rather than seek a legal solution; presumably, alternative procedures will provide access to help for a greater number of persons.

There has often been heated debate about the efficacy of various procedures in resolving disputes (for example see Felstiner, 1974, 1975 vs. Danzig and Lowy, 1975; also see Nader, 1980) and about the need for them. Much of the debate involves questions for which we do not have adequate empirical data. Does legal procedure transform and exacerbate conflict and to what extent? How do litigants view the legal process? Are there 'missing plaintiffs' who avoid the legal system but who would avail themselves of alternative means of third-party help if it were available? What are the social and psychological

*Preparation of this paper was supported, in part, by grants from the Donner Canadian Foundation and the Social Science and Humanities Research Council of Canada.
†University of Western Ontario, London, Canada.

costs of enduring problems? Do non-disputers handle their problems in ways that are different from disputers?

We have just begun a three-year study of the disputing process in one Canadian community that will address some of these questions. One project in the study will follow litigants through a small claims court. Recently, this court has instituted a pre-trial 'resolution hearing' procedure that appears to be a success, at least insofar as administrative efficiency is concerned. We will interview a sample of litigants at the time a dispute is entered, follow them through the resolution hearing and the trial, in the event that the resolution hearing is not successful, and do a follow-up interview some three to six months after the case is ended. A complementary project will draw a sample of persons from the same community from which the court draws its cases and attempt to discover how non-litigators with similar problems handle them without resort to legal action. Our theoretical approach will encompass analysis of variables at legal, sociological and social psychological levels.

In this paper I want to present some preliminary observations of the resolution hearings and describe some of the factors that may determine whether the hearings result in a settlement or proceed to trial. The first section presents a brief overview of alternative small claims court models. It helps to provide a comparative perspective on small claims court procedures. The following section describes the small claims court under study, with particular focus on the resolution hearing. The final section attempts to speculate on some of the social psychological and other variables associated with dispute dynamics that may explain resolution hearing outcomes.

Alternative Small Claims Procedures

Reviews of literature (see McGillis and Mullen, 1977; Ruhnka and Weller, 1978; Sander, 1977; Yngvesson and Hennessey, 1975) indicate that there are a number of procedural models that may be utilized in resolving small claims disputes. It is useful to consider each of them briefly and make some observations about each.

The traditional model for dealing with minor disputes is the adversary model whereby each party is responsible for developing his own case and placing it before a neutral judge. The judge operates under the procedural rules that are peculiar to the Anglo-American adversary system. While most small claims courts are supposed to operate on a modified adversary model, as will be described next, in fact in the Canadian courts I have observed the judge's training and habit often result in a return to the traditional model. The dispute is kept on the strict legal points at issue. The case is confined to a single adjudicators hearing; evidence in improper form is ruled inadmissible even though a delay might allow that evidence brought forth in proper form for consideration. The judge remains essentially passive during the presentation stage of the trial. This adversary model is less likely to be followed if both litigants are without legal counsel. However, if at least one of the litigants is represented by a lawyer or the case can be appealed the adversary rules are more likely to be followed. The philosophy underlying the adversary approach to proof-taking is well known and will not be elaborated here; Adams (1973) has set forth a defence of adversary procedure in small claims courts which follows the basic adversary system philosophy.

The model on which most Canadian small claims courts are based is a modified adversary model (see Yngvesson and Hennessey, 1975). While both parties remain responsible for developing their case and presenting it to the court, pleadings are simplified and the judge's role is modified so that he can take an active part in developing relevant evidence and/or attempting reconciliation between parties. The judge may take an active part in interrogating witnesses who are not articulate or who do not understand the substantive law. In the Ontario court we have under study, prior to the institution of the referee system, which will be discussed below, it was not at all unusual for the judge to ask litigants just before trial if they had attempted to talk and whether they should not step outside the courtroom and amicably settle their differences. The judge would play no part in these discussions, however. On the other hand the judge might attempt to effect some type of conciliation during the trial itself. The rationale behind the modified adversary model is that the basic qualities of adjudication are maintained, but litigants who are inexperienced with the legal system can utilize the court without hiring legal counsel. It should be noted that for the most part both the goals of providing help for the litigants and bringing about a negotiated settlement are overwhelmingly handicapped by the public and formal nature of the Canadian courtroom.

A third model is the arbitration model, which is utilized in a number of USA jurisdictions (see Sander, 1977). In some cases the arbitration hearing is virtually independent of the courtroom and compulsory, though the loser is allowed to appeal to a court for a trial *de novo*. In other jurisdictions, such as the New York small claims court studied and described by Sarat (1976), arbitration is elective and part of the normal court procedure. As the litigants appear in court they are given the option of formal public adjudication or of binding arbitration, carried out in private with a lawyer serving as the arbitrator. The assumption behind the arbitration is that away from the public eye and from the rules and 'battle' atmosphere of adversary adjudication more compromise solutions can be agreed upon, and cases can be resolved more efficiently as well.

Sarat's study shows some interesting results. Disputing parties who had a prior relational history were more likely to choose arbitration. Disputants who were not represented by counsel were also more likely to choose arbitration, but if either or both parties had retained counsel the choice was more likely to be adjudication. In comparing the decisions rendered Sarat found that disputes resolved by adjucation tended to be all-or-none whereas the arbitration decisions were more likely to be compromise solutions. Finally, Sarat surveyed litigants some months subsequent to their court appearance about the effect of the litigation on their relationship. Though the data were confounded because of the fact that the parties with a prior history were more likely to choose arbitration, the interesting finding was that fully 35 per cent of the parties in arbitration (9 per cent in adjudication) claimed the court experience had actually improved their relationship. The Sarat findings lend support to the notion that for some types of claims arbitration seems to be an effective alternative procedure. It should also be noted, though, that the New York model nevertheless requires the litigants to appear for trial in the courtroom, and the resolution is produced in a single appearance. The resolution of the dispute is an imposed decision rather than one negotiated by the parties, though the arbitrators do attempt to elicit the parties' suggestions and help.

Another model for resolving certain types of small claims disputes involves attempts at mediation and conciliation away from the legal setting. This approach, of course, has been utilized in some of the various neighbourhood justice centres in the USA (see McGillis and Mullen, 1977; Sander, 1977). Though intended primarily for minor criminal and domestic matters, some of the centres handle civil disputes as well. The basic approach is to provide, through a third party, the wherewithal to help the disputants develop and agree to their own solution to the problem, including, perhaps, a written agreement documenting the solution. While this model is useful for certain kinds of disputes, it has limited applicability for consumer, contract and tort cases. First, mediation requires the consent of the involved parties but there is often little incentive for the person allegedly owing the debt to pay up, and, moreover, there are few social pressures which can be applied to him or her to agree to the mediation effort. The centres recognize this fact and, for the most part, process disputes involving individuals, not institutions, and primarily involving only individuals who have had a relation to one another.

A final model combines advantages of mediation/conciliation with the regularized fact-finding of law. There are two stages to the model, entailing, first, a mediation or resolution hearing and, second, formal adjudication if the resolution hearing is not successful. Thus, the rationale behind this model is that some disputes are inappropriate for adjudication, or at least can be resolved without recourse to it. This is the model followed by the small claims court which we have under study and needs to be considered in more detail.

Resolution Hearings in a Small Claims Court

The small claims court under study is situated in a city of 250,000 and serves the rest of the county, composed of smaller towns and rural areas. Under Ontario statute the small claims court can handle claims up to $1,000 and any claim between $500 and $1,000 can be appealed. Both individual and corporate clients may use the court; a lawyer or some lay person may represent the litigants. Trials are held in a regular courtroom. The six regular County Court judges and one special judge preside over the court on a rotation basis.

Beginning about two years ago a pre-trial 'resolution hearing' was added to the court on an experimental basis, but it has now become a regular part of court procedure (and has been adopted by a number of other courts in urban centers in Ontario). Attendance at the hearing is not mandatory, but there are strong informal pressures that foster attendance. For example, members of the county bar were informed that the hearing would be standard procedure in a special 'practice direction' by the Senior County Court judge. Hearings are automatically scheduled for cases, with the exception of a few cases where attendance at the hearing might impose a hardship on one of the litigants (for example, if he or she lives out of the country). If one or both litigants fail to show up for the hearing it is automatically scheduled for trial.

The referee has no power to force anyone to give up his or her claim. If agreement is not reached in the hearing none of its proceedings will be admissible in court. The judges, incidentally, adhere strictly to these rules in the occasional instance that a party in the trial attempts to refer to something said in the resolution hearing. If a settlement between the parties is reached, the referee can have the agreement endorsed by a judge so that it has the same legal standing as a trial judgment.

There is only a single referee for the resolution hearings. He has no formal legal training but does have some unique qualifications that bear on his performance capabilities. He is a former police constable who also had a number of years experience as the Small Claims Court bailiff before being appointed as referee. As a former policeman he knows the city and the people well. This familiarity with the city and court procedure often intrude into the hearing in important ways. For example, in one dispute involving the facts of an automobile accident he was able to pinpoint the exact location and conditions of the accident and raise serious questions as to whether one of the disputant's version of the accident could be logically correct. His physical size and demeanor have also had a 'calming' effect in rare occurrences where the disputants have become emotional.

Hearings are scheduled for 30 minutes. The disputing parties, and their legal counsel, if any, meet with the referee in a comfortable private office in the court house. The parties are told that while they have a right to a trial the hearing is an attempt to define the issues and attempt to achieve settlement. The plaintiff is first asked to relate his or her side of the dispute. Sometimes the referee will interrupt and ask clarifying questions about the facts or about the relevance of the law. Then the defendant is asked to relate the other side of the dispute. The actions of the referee vary considerably, depending on such things as the factual or legal nature of the dispute, the attitudes of the disputants, and the absence or presence of legal counsel. For example, in complex factual disputes he may simply interrupt the hearing and indicate it should go directly to trial. In other cases he often suggests some form of settlement, that the parties should talk it over outside the hearing room, and that they should let him know within a few days whether they have settled or the case should be scheduled for trial. Persuasion attempts sometimes relate to the logic of the arguments and sometimes to probable trial outcomes. This is the case both when legal counsel are present or when they are absent, though the tone of the discussion may vary with presence/absence of legal counsel. In many cases persuasion attempts involve reminding the parties of the additional cost of time and money that going to trial will take: for example, 'You might spend a whole day in court waiting for your case to be heard; you should decide whether losing a day's work, and/or paying for a lawyer is worth it to you.' It should be noted that seldom does the referee assume the role of a therapeutic conciliator who attempts to reconcile the parties; rather the role is usually, and frequently exclusively, one of clarifying, providing information, and suggesting a settlement (see Yngvesson and Hennessey, 1975, pp. 257–262). Sometimes, the referee does perform other functions. He might suggest that a disputant should seek legal advice or he might attempt to suggest terms of payment when the issues involve ability to pay.

At least from an administrative point of view the resolution hearing appears quite successful. In 1979 the referee held 811 resolution hearings. Of these cases 325, or 40 per cent, were settled either in the resolution hearing itself or shortly following the resolution hearing. Another 246, or 30 per cent, were scheduled for trial. Of the remaining cases 135, or 17 per cent, were adjourned to a later date; 58, or 7 per cent, were adjourned *sine die*; and 47, or 6 per cent, were withdrawn. Many of the adjourned cases will have also resulted in settlement so that it is not unfair to estimate that the resolution hearing results in settlement of about 50 per cent of the cases.

There is one qualification to these statistics. Lawyers have apparently begun to use the resolution hearing in lieu of informal negotiations. Prior to the establishment of the resolution hearing, in cases where both parties had retained legal counsel, the lawyers would often initiate negotiations over the telephone or in person in an attempt to settle and avoid spending valuable time in court waiting for their client's case to be heard. But because the hearing is scheduled for a definite time, many lawyers now use the hearing as a point of first oral contact with the other side and as the vehicle for settlement negotiations. Thus, some of the cases settled in the hearing would probably have been settled without resort to trial anyway. At this point we do not have adequate data to suggest what percentage of cases these might be, though the percentage will not appreciably affect the general conclusion about the administrative success of the resolution hearing.

To digress slightly, it is worth noting that the use of the resolution hearing for purposes of negotiation may have some benefits for the disputing parties. Thibaut and Walker (1975, 1978) suggest that parties' perceived control over proceedings is positively related to their feelings that justice has been done. In the present instance rather than simply being informed of a deal worked out by their lawyers the parties are present at the negotiations and have a say in them. Thus, this unanticipated utilization of the resolution hearing by the lawyers on grounds of expediency may have produced a positive outcome with respect to subjective feelings about justice. This possibility will be investigated empirically as our research progresses.

Settlement and Non-settlement in the Resolution Hearings

One major question arising from the statistics about the resolution hearing involves the reasons why some cases are settled and others are not. Are there characteristics that predict resolution hearing outcome?

It should be noted from the outset that outcome or 'success' can refer to any number of criteria. Among these are the following:

Is the dispute settled or sent to trial?
What is the amount of the settlement and its form?
How do the parties perceive the fairness of the settlement?
How do the parties perceive the fairness of the hearing itself?
How does the remedy comport with legal criteria?

In our empirical research we hope to address all of these criteria, but for this essay we shall be concerned primarily with the first criterion, namely, whether the dispute is settled or not.

Disputes can be analysed according to their legal and other objective characteristics, their sociological characteristics and their social psychological characteristics. The latter analysis views disputes from the perspective of the disputing parties and considers their motives and other factors which affect decision making. Each of these levels of analysis may be useful in understanding the outcome of a legal dispute.

Legal Characteristics

Disputes may be categorized according to the type of legal claim (for example, torts, breach of contract, consumer disputes, debts, landlord–tenant disputes). Our initial impressions are that these categories are not strongly, if at all, related to outcome of the resolution hearings, with one major exception. Disputes involving the amount or terms of a wage garnishment or other payment agreement are usually settled in the hearing. In these the debt has been established by a court judgment or by the defendants' admission of liability; the only disagreement is ability to pay or amount to be paid within certain time periods. This kind of dispute tends to be settled by the resolution hearing.

Disputes can also be categorized according to other descriptive criteria: the amount of money involved; the complexity of the factual evidence; the number of parties to the suit; the status of the parties (that is, whether they are individuals or institutions, private citizens or business persons); the absence or presence of a countersuit; the absence or presence of legal counsel (and also whether the counsel is a lawyer or an articling student acting for the law firm). Disputes involving complex and conflicting factual evidence or disagreement about the applicability of a law are less likely to be resolved in the hearing. The presence of a countersuit probably also predicts the case will go to trial. Countersuits, however, often reflect intense affective conflict, or ego involvement, in the dispute, a factor to be considered at the social psychological level of analysis. Our initial observations hint that presence or absence of lawyers (either by only one or by all parties) is not related to settlement, or at least not very strongly so.

The sociological level of analysis shifts the focus away from the case itself to the parties and elements of their relationship to one another, as well as to the broader context in which the dispute takes place. Anthropological studies of other cultures, for example, suggest that the relationship between the disputants is an important predictor of resolution forum choice and outcome. Relationships that are 'multi-plex' vs. 'uni-plex' (that is, involving more than one role vs. a single role), are more likely to be resolved by mediation than adjudication (see, for example, Nader, 1975; Nader and Todd, 1978). Thus, a business dispute between relatives, who have to interact in other contexts, is more likely to be preferred and to be dealt with more constructively in an informal meeting than in adjudication. Similarly, disputants with a prior history or an expected future relationship are more likely to be amenable to mediation or other less formal procedures than disputants with no prior relationship. Recall that Sarat (1976) found that when given a choice disputants with a prior relationship, in comparison to those with no prior relationship, were more likely to choose arbitration over adjudication. Moreover, those choosing arbitration were more likely to subsequently report that the proceedings actually improved their relationship.

These above findings are interesting but may not be as applicable for the court that we are studying. Initial observations suggest that in many disputes characterized by a prior relationship it appears to be ruptured beyond repair when they reach the resolution hearing. However, perhaps the type of prior relationship and its duration may be related to resolution outcome; but, as yet, there is no suggested pattern in our data.

Other research suggests that the cultural context affects preference for procedure, that is sub-cultural values may influence attitudes for or against adjudication (see Gallanter, 1974; Nader, 1975). But such findings are not so germane to the present context where, in fact, one or both of the litigants has already opted for litigation and the other has elected to dispute the case. There is some indication that ethnic background of the disputants may predict whether the dispute will be resolved in the hearing, but the effects of ethnicity may be best understood as giving rise to certain social psychological attitudes. This brings us, then, to the third level of analysis.

Social Psychological Factors

A social psychological level of analysis looks at the dispute from the perspective of the disputing parties. What are their goals in the dispute? How do they assess costs and benefits in making decisions about options open to them? What situational and dispositional factors influence their assessment of benefits and costs? Disputes are complicated phenomena, and what follows is not a systematic integration of all the many variables involved but only an outline of some of the basic dynamics and parameters of disputes. Nevertheless, they suggest hypotheses regarding whether disputes will be settled or not.

Goals in Disputes

There appear to be many reasons for pursuing a dispute and many of these may not involve justice motives, at least not justice motives in the sense that they are traditionally conceptualized in social psychology (see Vidmar, 1981). Sometimes a plaintiff has multiple goals and, of course, the goal or goals of the defendant too affect the outcome. At this point we do not have a systematic classification scheme for these goals but some case examples help to suggest the diversity of goals and their relationship to resolution hearing outcome.

Because the Ontario Small Claims Court Act allows institutional plaintiffs, it is used as a debt-collecting agency. The agents of finance companies, the Public Utilities Commission etc., routinely file claims for uncollected debts. The attitudes of these agents are, more or less, impersonal and based on expediency. They will normally attempt to settle in the resolution hearing, if at all possible, simply to avoid spending time in court. A number of small business owners use the court in a similar manner. In other cases individual parties have a grievance of one sort or the other, but their primary goal is to get restitution and be done with the matter. If at all possible they too will settle. This basic attitude was epitomized in the case of two businessmen who had occasional past dealings with one another but had a disagreement about fulfillment of contractual obligations involving $300.00. While one had consulted a lawyer both appeared alone at the resolution hearing. The exchange was personal and friendly. The dispute was over facts and the two parties had agreed to disagree. Without articulating their attitudes *per se* they seemed to be saying 'We can't decide'. When the referee suggested that his interpretation of the facts was favourable to the defendant, both parties accepted it and agreed to settle. This general attitude sometimes characterizes disputes between strangers as well. The hearing, therefore, is sometimes approached as a problem-solving procedure, and the disputants' attitudes are to dispense with the matter as expeditiously as possible. *Ceteris paribus*, the parties will attempt to settle.

In other cases, however, the goals and behaviour of one or both of the disputing parties are more ego-involved, either in the sense that the dispute is seen as a personal attack on integrity or that it infringes on important values. Jones was not satisfied with auto repairs, engaged in a strong argument with the repair shop owner, and subsequently stopped payment on his cheque for $198.00. The owner retaliated by filing in court and having Jones' car impounded. Jones filed a countersuit alleging improper repair. Jones then retained a lawyer and recruited a professional mechanic as an expert witness. The resolution hearing was unsuccessful. The day the case was brought to trial lawyers tried again to obtain settlement, and the shop owner agreed on a slightly reduced bill of $150.00. Jones was informed by his lawyer that there was no chance whatsoever of winning and that legal fees for a day in court would be extensive. Jones insisted on a trial anyway. As predicted, he lost and with legal fees, court costs and the repair bill, his expenses – excluding a day off work for him and his wife – were well over $500.00. A dispute involving White was lower in affect and less personal but equally non-rational in simple economic terms. White is an apartment owner known for his conservative views. A dispute arose with the Public Utilities Commission over a $90.00 electric bill and the PUC sued. At the resolution hearing White was most cordial. He conceded to having had similar disputes with the PUC in the past, losing all of them in court; he admitted probable legal liability for the debt and acknowledged he would lose in court. In the course of the discussion the PUC agents discovered they could legally demand a $5,000 commercial security deposit and said they were likely to do so if White persisted. White openly asserted that he wanted to go to trial because 'At least, you [PUC] gentlemen will be forced to earn your money'. White's goal seemed to be his desire to assert the values of free enterprise and individualism in protest against government rules.

Two other disputes that were not resolved in the resolution hearing illustrate other goals pursued in disputes. Smith had a televison repaired at Werner's shop. Though the shop recommended a full overhaul of the set, estimated at a cost of $150.00, Smith authorized repairs of $52.00. Upon taking the set home Smith was dissatisfied; he telephoned and argued with Werner, and then cancelled the $52.00 cheque. Despite being angry Werner was prepared to write the bill off and be done with it. In the meantime, however, Smith complained to the Better Business Bureau. Werner interpreted this act as a slur on his business reputation. He proceeded to file in the small claims court, would not settle in the resolution hearing, and spent four hours in court with legal counsel waiting for the case to be heard. When interviewed after winning the case, Werner clearly expressed the belief that only a trial could have cleared his business reputation. The goals of specific and general deterrence were paramount in the case of Williams, a car dealer. Williams pressed a $400.00 claim against three agents for an insurance company. He argued they had violated an oral agreement to pay him for the use of a car loaned to a customer while the customer's damaged car was being repaired. The relationship between the dealer and the insurance company agents was of nearly 15 years standing and, because of the interdependent nature of their respective businesses, must necessarily continue in the future. There had been many misunderstandings with this company before, as well as with agents of other insurance companies, and the dealer attempted to use litigation as a means of helping clarify obligations. He refused to settle in the resolution hearing because, in his view, he wanted these particular agents, and other agents, to honour perceived obligations. He believed a judicial decision would help to achieve that end, whereas settlement in a resolution hearing would not. Whether the dealer was correct or not in his assumptions, and even whether there was some ego-involvement in the dispute as well, his goals of deterrence help to explain the refusal to settle.

Of course, a particular disputant may have more than one goal and two parties involved in a dispute may each have separate goals. The case examples also suggest something else, namely that disputant goals may change in the time period between the inception of conflict and appearance in the legal system. In particular ego involvement in the dispute may increase to the point where one or both of the disputants are seeking personal vindication rather than a solution to a perceived economic inequity.

But is understanding of disputant goals sufficient to explain outcome? No. Many disputes characterized by considerable degrees of ego-involvement are settled during or after the resolution hearing. And with respect to the cases where the dispute is primarily about equity one is inclined to ask why the parties, if they are reasonable, do not get together without resort to law in the first place.

The Role of Information and Transaction Cost Estimation in Dispute Settlement

Observation of the resolution hearings and the post-hearing interviews reveal two other important impressions bearing on the social psychology of the dispute process. First, the disputing parties frequently lack information or have misinformation about each other's side of the dispute. Often, the un-covering of these facts changes the whole nature of the dispute. Second, the parties have frequently underestimated the costs of continuing the dispute but growing awareness of these costs fosters the desire to settle. Leff (1970) has developed an economic perspective on commerical transactions that addresses both of these issues and is probably applicable to torts and other disputes as well. Leff's analysis will be summarized, and then some observations about its relevance to dispute settlement in this particular court will be tendered.

In Leff's (1970) analysis the genesis of a dispute is when a creditor requests a debtor to pay up, but either because of unwillingness or inability (for example, lack of funds) the debtor does not do so. If the matter were as simple as that the solution to the stand-off would be simple coersion. In the case of the unwilling debtor the law could simply force the debtor to pay up and in the case of the unable debtor there would be no need because there is no chance of collecting even if coersion is used. Unfortunately, the information flow between creditor and debtor is often unclear, and, what is equally important, there are transac-tion costs involved with the collection of debt, costs which are borne by both parties. The creditor has to take time off to file in court, to perhaps seek the aid of a lawyer, to spend a day in court, to pay filing fees and if she/he loses, perhaps pay the costs of the debtor. For the debtor there are transaction costs which go beyond merely having to pay the debt. He or she has to also bear the costs of time in court and associated expenditures, to perhaps be deprived of goods that are of more value to him/her than the creditor, to risk a blot on self reputation, that is to be known as a bad credit risk, to have wages garnisheed and so forth. If, in fact, both creditor and debtor could know and accurately calculate these transaction costs ahead of time – and if they were rational persons – they could resolve the dispute by compromising on some figure that took these transaction costs into account.

Leff acknowledges, however, that there is another element involved in calculating the impact of transaction costs, an element which he conveniently summarizes as 'spite', and which we have referred to already as ego-involvement. From his economic perspective spite can be operationalized as a situation where one partly will hurt himself to hurt another more. Leff also recognizes the motive of 'superspite' whereby a party will hurt himself a lot simply to hurt the other party a little. Spite is an important element in disputes and, indeed, people are willing to pay to satisfy an urge to spite. Nevertheless, Leff argues, persuasively, that spite too can be translated into economic terms and its value is usually a finite sum: 'While it has some value for almost everyone, the more it costs the less likely it is to be bought' (Leff, 1970, p. 19). In concrete terms a creditor may be willing to spend $300 to gain $50 but it is unlikely that to gain the $50 she/he will mortgage his or her business, house and the family car. At a certain point in the dispute the economic realities of spite become recognized, though it may be advantageous to keep the other party in the dark about what the costs really are.

From this analysis, Leff argues that many, perhaps most, disputes are based upon lack of information about the reality of the dispute and its attendant costs. For one thing a creditor who attempts to collect from a debtor on the verge of bankruptcy is wasting his or her time because even if the creditor wins, s/he cannot collect. For another, parties seldom if ever calculate the transaction costs accurately: these include the costs of legal proceedings in time and money; the value of spite, reputation and credibility for both parties; the ability of the debtor to pay and of the creditor to accept less; and the level of accuracy with which the opposing party is able to calculate all of the above. Since distortion of reality by either or both parties escalates the dispute and may ultimately cause more harm than can be gained, Leff (1970, p. 40) argues that it is in the interest of both parties to 'increase each other's level of accurate information, and to facilitate the efficient mutual use of that information'. The difficulty in many transactions, however, is that often there are no channels of communication between creditor and debtor, or they are not used. Leff argues, therefore, that a mandatory pre-adjudication hearing would help to increase information flow and avoid the need for many trials.

Leff's analysis of dispute dynamics appears to fit many of the cases observed in our pilot research and, moreover, his prescription for a pre-adjudication hearing is essentially fulfilled by the resolution hearing. However, two issues merit elaboration regarding social psychological dynamics.

There are, for example, different reasons for the information/misinformation gap between parties, depending on the type of case. Where the plaintiff is an institution or an agent of some business (such as a bank, a finance company or a collection agency) that lack of information-finding can be ascribed to bureaucratic efficiency motives involved in routine debt processing. Agents for such plaintiffs do not have, or at least want to take, time to discover if the defendant has good reason for the dispute. Investigating each case and negotiating with each party is economically inefficient. By treating every case as if the defendant is liable these agents induce the vast majority of debtors to pay up, often before a resolution hearing is scheduled. For the remainder it is more efficient to leave information gathering for the resolution hearing rather than attempt to make informal contacts and negotiate with the defendant. In such cases the agent, upon ascertaining the other side's position, may decide there is a quick and easy solution and withdraw the case or agree to terms which the defendant was seeking in the first place.

Disputes between private individuals are often lacking in information for other reasons. Interviews with disputants indicate that many disputes proceed rapidly to high affect and ego-involvement between the parties, and, consequently, the disputants fail to communicate calmly and rationally. In a word the parties do not listen to one another. The problem is exacerbated when the parties blow off steam or seek intellectual or emotional support by telling their side of the story to friends, co-workers and spouses. Naturally, these other persons are selected for their sympathetic ear and hear only one side of the story. They react by providing social support and reinforce the belief that this version of the story is correct; frequently these other persons actively encourage legal action. As a result, no further communication takes place until the resolution hearing. The additional facts brought out at the hearing, however, create a new perception of the dispute which frequently fosters settlement.

A second point of elaboration concerns the transactions costs which Leff has elaborated. We have already noted that agents engaged in routine debt collecting are well aware of these costs and calculate them rationally. They are also known and calculated by persons who have been in court before, the so-called 'repeat players' (Gallanter, 1974). First-time litigants who have obtained legal counsel have usually begun to develop some awareness of these costs prior to the hearing, simply through discussion of counsel fees and the possibility of court costs. It is the unrepresented litigant who usually comes face to face with these costs in their entirety for the first time at the resolution hearing. For many this aspect of the dispute is a sobering experience, explicitly aided, as we noted earlier, by the comments of the referee.

Structuring of Legal Reality by the Referee.

The discussion of the role of information relevant to the substance of the dispute and the growing awareness of transaction costs assumes veridicality of the information. The referee's job is to elicit that information and the assumption is that the parties will then make informed decisions based on that information. However, for inexperienced litigants without legal counsel the referee also serves as a reference source for interpreting those facts and, not infrequently, interpreting the relevant law. In brief the referee unavoidably assumes the role of defining legal reality with respect to the law itself and to the strength and direction of the evidence. Despite his cautions that the hearing is not a trial and that he has no authority to impose a decision, inevitably he is defined as an authority by some litigants. And just as inevitably, some of those litigants without knowledge, experience, or confidence may agree to a settlement primarily on the basis of that perceived authority. This fact, of course, is relevant to criticisms that the hearing becomes a quasi-trial, that cases may be decided by hidden rules, that parties may be subtly coerced into settlement. Whether one accepts or rejects the merits of these criticisms, however, the strong possibility remains that some cases may be settled solely on the definition of legal reality provided by the referee.

Some Concluding Observations

In this paper I have attempted to provide a sketch of the disputing process with respect to one single small claims court, which uses both a resolution hearing and adjudication as a means of settling disputes. The observations are based upon unsystematic pilot data and can only be considered tentative. Nevertheless, they paint a picture of the disputing process as a complex phenomenon that must be studied at various levels of analysis and all are necessary to explain dispute outcomes. In particular it is necessary to view the dispute from the perspective of the disputing parties and consider their motives, knowledge, assessment of transaction costs and degree of dependence on others to define evidentiary and legal reality.

Our discussion has attempted only to tender some reasons why disputes may or may not be settled in the resolution hearing. Data about the extent to which these various factors are relevant to the universe of cases handled in the court remain to be collected. The other criteria, such as perceptions of fairness of outcomes and procedures by which the legal process may be judged, are equally important, though they have not been discussed here. Understanding of these various processes will eventually help us to predict the success of similar procedures in other contexts. For instance, even though the data suggest the resolution hearing is an administrative success in this court, there is some anecdotal evidence that it is not always so successful when utilized in other jurisdictions. Is success or lack of it a function of particular referees, of the nature of the cases brought to the hearing, of characteristics of disputants that vary from jurisdiction to jurisdiction, of certain administrative considerations varying between jurisdictions, or some combination of these? Answers to these questions will, hopefully, be forthcoming at the end of the research project.

References

Adams, G. (1973), 'The small claims court and the adversary process: More problems of function and form', *The Canadian Bar Review*, **51**, 583–616.

Danzig, R. and Lowy, M. (1975), 'Everyday disputes and mediation' *Law and Society Review*, **9**, 675–684.

Felstiner, W. (1974), 'Influences of social organization on dispute processing', *Law and Society Review*, **9**, 63–94.

Felstiner, W. (1975), 'Avoidance as dispute processing', *Law and Society Review*, **9**, 695–706.

Gallanter, M. (1974), 'Why the "haves" come out ahead: Speculations on the limits of legal change', *Law and Society Review*, **9**, 95–160.

Leff, A. (1970), 'Injury, ignorance, and spite – the dynamics of coercive collection', *Yale Law Journal*, **80**, 1–46.

McGillis, D. and Mullen, J. (1977), *Neighborhood Justice Centers: An Analysis of Potential Models*, U.S. Department of Justice, Washington, D.C.

Nader, L. (1975), 'Forums for justice: A cross-cultural perspective', *Journal of Social Issues*, **31**, 151–170.

Nader, L. (ed.) (1980), *No Access to Law*, Academic Press, New York.

Nader, L. and Todd, H. (eds) (1978), *The Disputing Process: Law in Ten Societies*, Columbia University Press, New York.

Ruhnka, J. and Weller, S. (1978), *Small Claims Courts: A National Examination*, National Center for State Courts, Williamsburg.

Sander, F. (1977), *Report on the National Conference on Minor Disputes Resolution*, American Bar Foundation, Chicago.

Sarat, A. (1976), 'Alternatives in dispute processing: Litigation in a small claims court', *Law and Society Review*, **10**, 339–376.

Thibaut, J. and Walker, L. (1975), *Procedural Justice: A Psychological Analysis*, Erlbaum Associates, Hillsdale, N. J.

Thibaut, J. and Walker, L. (1978), 'A theory of procedure', *California Law Review*, **66**, 541–566.

Vidmar, N. (1981), 'Justice motives and other psychological factors in the development and resolution of disputes', in Lerner, M. and Lerner, S. (eds), *The Justice Motive in Social Behaviour*, Plenum, New York.

Yngvesson, B. and Hennessey, P. (1975), 'Small claims, complex disputes: A review of the small claims literature', *Law and Society Review*, **9**, 219–274.

Factors Affecting Success in the Mediation of Legal Disputes: Third Party Conciliation through the German 'Schiedsmann'[1]

GÜNTER BIERBRAUER*

Conflicts between human beings are sometimes settled by the intervention of a third party. The activity of third parties may range from the informal mediation of a dispute between friends, through the therapeutic or quasi-therapeutic intervention of a marriage counsellor to the legally based intervention of a judge, who, in his official capacity within the judicial system, is charged by society to play the role of a mediator or adjudicator.

Despite its importance for or in the maintenance of social peace, the role of third parties in resolving interpersonal conflicts has been rather neglected in empirical research. Although social psychologists have been very active in the past in studying interpersonal conflicts, they have nevertheless focused their research on two basic paradigms. According to Rubin and Brown (1975) almost half of the studies described in the more than 1000 publications on dispute settlement appearing between 1960 and 1975 were based either on the prisoners' dilemma game or related experimental games. Besides the lack of external validity inherent in these paradigms (see Sermat, 1970; Dorris, 1972) the overemphasis on experimental games may have led to a neglect of equally important modes of conflict management.

The study to be reported was aimed at investigating the role and the effectiveness of third parties in legal disputes. In an empirical pilot study the activity of the German *Schiedsmann* (that is, 'mediator') served as a paradigm for the investigation of techniques used by third parties in actual conflict situations.

---

*University of Osnabrück, West Germany.

The *Schiedsmann's* Legal Status and the Scope of his Activities

In Germany, the *Schiedsmann* is a public but extrajudicial institution for the settlement of legally based private disputes. A *Schiedsmann* is elected to his honorary office by the organs of his respective municipal or district government for a period of 5 years or longer. He must be at least 30 years of age and live in the area where he holds his office. No specific training for the office is required, although he may participate in regional training seminars which are organized from time to time both by the local jurisdiction and the Federal *Schiedsmann* Association.

The competence of the *Schiedsmann* extends both to criminal and civil disputes. His activities in the area of criminal law are restricted to the offenses described in Section 380 of the German Code of Criminal Procedure, namely, breaches of domestic peace, minor intentional or negligent bodily injuries, the uttering of threats, property damage, breaches of confidentiality and insults. For these offenses, the injured party may seek criminal sanctions against the accused party by means of a private suit *only* after a reconciliation attempt before the *Schiedsmann* has failed. The reconciliation proceeding (*Sühneverfahren*) in a criminal case has the aim of bringing about a settlement between the parties by providing the plaintiff with satisfaction for the wrong done to him, in return for which he abandons his right to seek criminal sanctions.

The *Schiedsmann's* competence in the area of civil disputes is restricted to actions involving pecuniary claims. At present, however, only approximately every thirtieth proceeding before the *Schiedsmann* concerns a civil dispute.

Proceedings take place in the presence of both parties, generally at the *Schiedsmann's* private residence. Although the defendant is obliged to appear before the *Schiedsmann*, he cannot be compelled to do so, nor to take part in the actual negotiations, and, in addition, he can reject any proposal made for settlement.

While the use of an authorized representative (*Bevollmächtigter*) is precluded, a party may bring along an adviser (*Beistand*) for support. The *Schiedsmann*, however, may dismiss such advisers – with the exception of statutory legal representatives and lawyers – at any stage of the proceeding. He may also hear witnesses and experts who appear voluntarily. If parties reach an agreement, its terms are recorded in the register; otherwise, the failure of the reconciliation attempt is noted.

In the event of a reconciliation in a criminal case, the plaintiff abandons his right to institute criminal proceedings. In return, the accused gives him satisfaction in the form of an apology, for example, by donating money to a public or charitable cause, by compensating for real damages or pain and suffering, or even simply by making partial or total payment of the costs of the reconciliation proceeding. The settlement may be legally enforced.

Reconciliation proceedings necessarily make it more difficult for the petitioner to secure his full claims, since he often has to yield in some way or other to bring about a settlement. Both parties must therefore be interested in agreeing to find a compromise solution in order to make mediation possible. As a result, the success of the proceedings depends on the ability of the *Schiedsmann* to make the parties understand that it is in their common interest to reach a settlement.

Irrespective of their legal definitions, the disputes which must be brought before a *Schiedsmann* prior to reaching a court are generally of a type which cannot be precisely defined normatively. The social significance, context, and consequences of 'insult' and 'breach of domestic peace' can scarcely be defined by statute.

Method and Data

Although the office of the *Schiedsmann* is formally tied to the statutory framework of the criminal and civil law, the actual method of the proceedings is left to the *Schiedsmann's* own preference. To this extent, this study offered an opportunity to determine quantitatively those variables that in real conflict situations make a difference between success or failure of third party intervention. Admittedly, it would have been desirable to observe the behaviour in actual reconciliation attempts. However, this proved unfeasible because of the nonpublic character of these proceedings. Thus, we had to confine ourselves to the data available from a questionnaire which essentially asked for mediatory behaviour and furthermore tapped the attitudes of the *Schiedsmänner* towards their office.[2]

A total of 218 *Schiedsmänner* (142 from the jurisdiction of the Bielefeld District Court and 76 from the jurisdiction of the Bonn District Court) were sent questionnaires, 101 of which were returned in a usable condition. Since the study was only exploratory, our hypothesis formation was guided by a relatively great number of variables.

In general, data on the following two classes of variables were recorded and each related to the outcome of reconciliation proceedings:
(1)   Data referring to quantifiable aspects of the proceedings, for example, the number of cases handled by the *Schiedsmann* or his time in office.
(2)   Data reflecting the attitudes of the *Schiedsmann* towards his work and his social environment.

Results

In this part of the study our analysis was guided by the question as to what are the characteristics of third party intervention that make the difference between successful and unsuccessful mediation outcomes.

Social Status of the 'Schiedsmann' within his Jurisdiction

The effectiveness of the *Schiedsmann* seems to be decisively dependent upon his social status within his area of jurisdiction. Seventy-five per cent of the *Schiedsmänner* in rural areas claimed to know more than half or almost all parties personally, as against 52 per cent of those in suburban districts and 23 per cent of those in cities. Furthermore, the degree of personal familiarity with the parties increased with the *Schiedsmann's* time in office. Fifty per cent of the *Schiedsmänner* who had been in office for 5 years or less stated that they knew more than half, or almost all, parties personally. This was true for 61 per cent of those in office between 5 and 10 years and for 63 per cent of those in office for more than 10 years. The question remains open whether this increase was due to contacts of an official nature or to other factors.

The rate of success – expressed as the ratio between the total number of reconciliation proceedings conducted in 1974[3] and the number of those which were successfully settled – increased with the degree of the *Schiedsmann's* personal familiarity with the parties. For instance, those *Schiedsmänner* who indicated that they knew 23 per cent of the parties personally, obtained a success rate up to 55 per cent. However, those who indicated that they knew 54 per cent of the parties personally had a success rate of 70 per cent and more.

If personal familiarity plays such a decisive role in successful reconciliation proceedings, the *Schiedsmann's* execution of his office may be characterized as an informal, though not private, form of dispute resolution. This is supported by the fact that, according to their own self-characterization, 90 per cent of those questioned thought that their personal skills in resolving disputes, such as empathy, ability to listen etc., was more important for reaching a successful settlement than exact observance of the statutory provisions in the *Schiedsmann's* Ordinance.

Since the *Schiedsmann* has no specific expert knowledge, it is perhaps his recognition in his jurisdiction and his familiarity with the activities of his fellow citizens that legitimize his mediatory intervention in the social relationships of the parties. At any rate, the *Schiedsmänner* questioned only occasionally gave as a reason for their appointment to office such characteristics as conciliatory ability, neutrality, etc., but, instead, overwhelmingly mentioned their recognition in the area and in local government and administration, their good reputation, and the respect and trust the population had for them.

Inclusion of Underlying Causes

As a rule, the actual dispute which brings the parties before the *Schiedsmann* is not an isolated incident. An open discussion by the parties makes it possible to give consideration to the underlying causes of the dispute in the settlement arrangement. In fact, those *Schiedsmänner* who, by their own assertions, regularly incorporated such causes in the proceedings, had a higher rate of success than those who confined themselves mainly to the specific dispute before them (70 per cent, as against 55 per cent).

Social Therapeutic Service vs Administrative and Bureaucratic Proceedings

With respect to the understanding of their role, two ideal types of *Schiedsmänner* might be defined. A person who sees his work primarily as a social-therapeutic service (S-type) may be distinguished from another person, who regards his work primarily as an official administrative and bureaucratic function at the lowest level of the legal system (A-type).

A *Schiedsmann's* commitment to social therapy was characterized by the following variables:

(a)   Proceedings of longer than average duration.

(b)   More frequent than average contacts with the accused party outside the actual reconciliation proceedings.

(c)   A more frequent than average calling of witnesses to appear at the reconciliation hearing.

(d)   Incorporation of the underlying causes of the dispute and not restricting the proceedings to the specific dispute at issue.

(e)   Positive self-evaluation as a mediator in comparison to court adjudication.

Each variable in the above list specifies a characteristic assigned to the S-type and, for the purpose of our study, was scored 1. The opposite characteristic in each case (proceedings of shorter than average duration etc.) was assigned to the A-type and was scored 0.

The *Schiedsmänner* who scored lowest on a scale of 0–5, that is, with a score from 0 to 1, most closely corresponded to the A-type. Their average rate of success was 52 per cent (see Note 3). In contrast, the *Schiedsmänner* who scored from 3 to 5 and as such corresponded most closely to the S-type, obtained a success rate of 74 per cent.

Thus, proceedings before the *Schiedsmänner* assigned to the S-type were apparently better suited for resolving disputes.

Moreover, *Schiedsmänner* who were concerned primarily with helping other people and with endeavouring to secure a settlement and understanding between the parties (assigned to the S-type) differed in their behaviour from the *Schiedsmänner* who were primarily interested in formal success in the sense of the *Schiedsmann* Ordinance (assigned to the A-type). Proceedings before the first group, according to the *Schiedsmänner's* own estimate, had a considerably longer average duration than those interested only in formal success. In addition, the first group of *Schiedsmänner* more clearly preferred the procedural precepts of allowing the parties to speak their minds thoroughly, even if voices were raised, and of letting the parties find a solution themselves through their discussions, in contrast to the opposing precepts of requiring discipline in the proceedings and of proposing solutions to the parties even at an early stage. According to their own statements, 76 per cent of them regularly incorporated the underlying causes of the disputes into the proceedings, as against 47 per cent of the *Schiedsmänner* interested only in formal success. However, it must be noted that this descriptive presentation mainly rests on the subjective statements of the *Schiedsmänner* questioned, and, therefore may say more about a *Schiedsmann's* own evaluation of his work than about his actual behaviour in reconciliation proceedings.

Multivariate Analysis of the 'Schiedsmann' Questionnaire

In order to go beyond the descriptive relationships and to determine the strength of the observed regularities, the following correlations between a number of selected variables and rate of success were found to be significant at least at the 0.05-level (see Note 3):

(1) Degree of personal familiarity ($r = 0.27$).
(2) Inclusion of underlying causes ($r = 0.34$).
(3) Increase of settlement rate with time in office ($r = 0.21$).
(4) Liberal attitudes toward political and social values ($r = 0.21$).

Retention of a lawyer in reconciliation proceedings correlates negatively ($r = -0.21$) with rate of success, that is, the participation of a lawyer tended to make a settlement less probable.

Furthermore, a multiple regression analysis was performed, based on 25 variables as predictors from the *Schiedsmann* questionnaire which were meaningful for this purpose. If we define rate of success as the criterion, then, by using multiple regression, we can determine how much variance can be predicted by the characteristics surveyed, such as duration of proceedings, attitudes etc. The highest amount of variance is accounted for by the variable 'degree of personal familiarity with the parties', namely 8 per cent. The next highest contribution of 7 per cent is attributable to the variable 'inclusion of underlying causes in the handling of dispute'. The contribution of other variables which might be expected to exist on the basis of our intuition, for example, the frequency of participation in *Schiedsmann* training seminars, or the length of time active as a *Schiedsmann*, had a negligible influence on the rate of success.

In summary, it may be said that the successful *Schiedsmann* could attribute part of his higher rate of success to his familiarity with the parties' personal situations and to the fact that, according to his own statements, he regularly incorporated the underlying causes of the dispute in his proceedings. Moreover, a liberal attitude towards social and political values appears to have a positive influence on his activity. On the other hand, social and structural aspects, such as time in office, knowledge of formal legal aspects etc., were possibly overrated as factors contributing towards a successful execution of the job.

Discussion

It may be true that the office of the *Schiedsmann* occupies a marginal position in the administration of justice in Germany and that it plays only a minor role. From the point of view of legal theory, however, the institution is of importance at least insofar as its structure and functioning throw light on the possibilities and limits of conflict management through mediation. In the future, mediation as a specific method of dealing with disputes will probably become a more important topic of discussion among legal scholars. In the USA this discussion has already begun, and new types of 'mediation agencies' have been established in several cities (see Danzig and Lowy, 1975, for a survey of this development).

The mediator attempts to gain influence by addressing the interests of the parties. The obligatory reconciliation attempt compels the parties – before having their dispute decided by a judge in private criminal proceedings as a conflict of values – to seek a compromise solution in proceedings where their conflict is treated as one of interests. The aim of these proceedings is for the parties jointly to find a conciliatory solution with regard to the future, and not for a third party to examine a set of facts from the past and to decide who is in the right. The task of the third party engaged in reconciliation proceedings is to remove the conflict from the realm of abstract principles ('de-ideologization' of the conflict), particularly by pointing out the unfavourable consequences a private criminal suit might have for both sides, and to draw the attention of the parties to areas of common interest.

For questions involving merely interests, the barriers to compromise are not so strong as for questions involving justice or truth (Eckhoff, 1966), which, because of their binary division into just and unjust, truth and falsehood, allow no room for the intermediate positions necessary for compromise. Moreover, the encouragement of a compromise increases respect for the mediator's impartiality, and makes him appear as a moderate and reasonable man with an ability to look at the problem from various points of view. He is thus contrasted to the parties, who often appear to be one-sided and contentious, since they cannot themselves succeed in resolving the conflict (Aubert, 1963).

It is characteristic of the *Schiedsmann's* field of activity that he regularly has to deal with socially or psychologically highly complex conflicts on a face-to-face basis without reference to clear legal norms, rather than with conflicts of low complexity in situations where such clear legal norms exist, such as the purchase of goods. A highly complex conflict implies that all expectations between the partners involved in the interaction are potentially relevant to the conflict (Gessner, 1976).

In private criminal suits the original conflict (a conflict of interests) is transformed into a meta-conflict (a conflict of values), which may then be decided upon by a judge. The mechanism of judicial conflict resolution compels the parties to formulate their opposing interests as a disagreement concerning particular facts in the past or legal standards or both (Aubert, 1963). As a result, the needs of the parties and their wishes for the future are no longer of decisive importance for the resolution of the conflict.

Resolvability is brought about through the use of a legal language filter by reducing social reality to a normative structure according to the legal criteria of relevance. The judge, who is more or less bound by normative rules of decision-making, can take into account the pecularities of the situation and the parties involved only with great difficulty. Only a very small segment of the relationship to be decided upon, namely that which is legally relevant, comes before him for consideration. In the case of conflicts which revolve around legal standards anyway, the intervention of the judge ensures the observance of the rules on which the conflict is based. In such a case, the law is not brought in from the outside solely in order to simplify the complex realities of life, since it is already the direct subject of the dispute.

On the other hand, there are hardly any specific rules of decision-making concerning the conduct of the third party involved in reconciliation proceedings. As a result, the pecularities of the situation and of the parties can be taken into account to a considerable degree. Since the criteria for resolving the conflict are not fixed, reconciliation proceedings are appropriate for dealing with highly complex disputes. The parties involved can themselves determine the relevance of certain aspects of the dispute and, by mutually adjusting their demands, even ignore the past and be guided only by their wishes for a cooperative future.

One of the purposes of laws is to manoeuvre people into different behaviour patterns to those they would follow in the absence of such laws.

In these examples entry is under the author's name. Sometimes there is no author as such but an editor or compiler, and entry is then under his or her name:

[8] John Lubans, ed., *Progress in educating...*

Lubans, John, ed., *Progress in education...*

Sometimes the "author" is an organization of some kind:

Cardiff, Welsh Office

United Kingdom, Department of Education and Science

HOW TO DESCRIBE A PERIODICAL ARTICLE

(a) In a footnote

[7] Maurice B. Line, Requirements for library and information work and the role of library education, <u>Education for Information</u> 1 (March 1983), 27.

The pagination here refers, of course, to the whole article.

HOW TO DESCRIBE AN ESSAY WITHIN A COLLECTION

(a) In a footnote

[14] A. Maltby, "The educational role of the college library", <u>in College</u>

Notes

1 Dedicated to the memory of Klaus Koch, my collaborator on this project.
2 A second part of the study was based on a content analysis of 1000 official reconciliation records. These provided information on the subject matter of actual disputes handled, the parties involved etc. (see Bierbrauer, Falke and Koch, 1978).
3 In this and the subsequent analyses referring to the success rate only those *Schiedsmänner* are taken into account who had conducted at least six proceedings in 1974.

References

Aubert, V. (1963), 'Competition and dissensus: two types of conflict resolution', *Journal of Conflict Resolution*, **7**, 26–42.

Bierbrauer, G., Falke, J. and Koch, K. (1978), 'Conflict and its settlement: an interdisciplinary study concerning the legal basis, function and performance of the institution of the *Schiedsmann'*, in Cappelletti, M. and Weisner, J. (eds), *Access to Justice: Promising Institutions, Vol. 2*, Sijthoff/ Giuffrè Leyden/Milan pp. 40–101.

Danzig, R. and Lowy, M. J. (1975), 'Everyday disputes and mediation in the United States: A reply to Professor Felstiner', *Law and Society Review*, **9**, 675–694.

Dorris, J. W. (1972), 'Reactions to unconditional cooperation: a field study emphasizing variables neglected in laboratory research', *Journal of Personality and Social Psychology*, **22**, 387–397.

Eckhoff, T. (1966), 'The mediator, the judge and the administrator in conflict resolution', *Acta Sociologica*, **10**, 148–172.

Gessner, V. (1976), *Recht und Konflikt, Eine soziologishe untersuchung privatrechtlicher Konflikte in Mexiko*. Mohr and Siebeck, Tübingen.

Rubin, J. Z. and Brown, B. R. (1975), *The Social Psychology of Bargaining and Negotiation*, Academic Press.

Sermat, V. (1970), 'Is game behaviour related to behaviour in other interpersonal situations?', *Journal of Personality and Social Psychology*, **16**, 92–109.

On the Mental Element in Crime and Behaviourism

D. E. BLACKMAN*

The domain of mental life has been a constant problem for psychology. What is the role of our 'inner' lives in determining what we do, and how can the necessarily private events of our mental lives be captured in objective studies? Some commentators feel that the discipline of psychology has evaded these basic issues by redefining its original field of interest as the study of behaviour rather than the study of mental processes and by adopting an approach which is modelled unduly on the methods of the natural sciences. While psychologists have elaborated on environmental, social, physiological or genetic influences on behaviour, some feel that they have become detached from common sense explanations. Joynson (1974, p. 3) has suggested that 'the layman feels, most of the time, that he understands his own behaviour well enough. He almost always knows what he is doing, and why he is doing it'. He therefore argues that if we want to know why a person is behaving in a particular way, we need merely ask him or her. If we were to doubt the account we receive, we would be implying that the person is a fool, a liar or a hypocrite.

The natural science model of psychology has therefore come under attack: instead of seeking the causes of behaviour, psychologists have been urged to engage in a moral science of action which seeks the reasons for our conduct (for example, Shotter, 1975). One problem for this approach, however, is to be found in the fact that there are wide individual differences in people's abilities to bring to words a coherent account of their own actions. Is the relative inarticulacy so often shown in football crowds as opposed to seminar rooms, or the unelaborated explanation of their behaviour so often shown by criminals called to account for their conduct, necessarily to be regarded as the outcome of foolishness, deceit or hypocrisy?

---

*Professor of Psychology, University College, Cardiff

The criminal law in the United Kingdom is of course constantly confronted by this very issue. It is therefore constructive to consider how the process of law, which is based so explicitly on the articulation of common sense, comes to conclusions about the existence or absence of the mental element in crime which is often required by the specification of an offence (*mens rea*). 'An act does not make a man guilty of a crime unless his mind be also guilty', and so criminal law, though designed to influence what we do rather than what we think, is permeated by the need to interpret or attribute mental elements to which the accused person alone has direct access and which can therefore only be inferred by others from what he says or from the circumstances of the crime.

Kenny (1978) has used reports of legal cases to develop his thoughts on free will and responsibility as philosophical issues. He suggests that notions such as belief and intention are indispensable whenever we try to communicate with each other, including in the formal context of criminal proceedings. Kenny finds that:

. . . the reports of the courts and the decisions of judges provide a fund of material for philosophical study which is more concrete, vivid and credible, while at the same time more extraordinary and thought-provoking, than any product of philosophers' imaginations. Moreover, the needs of the courts to reach a decision, and the experience of legal systems over long periods of practical operation, have in some cases brought a precision into legal concepts which can contrast favourably with the achievements of philosophers. (p. 2)

Psychologists, whether of an empirical or an hermeneutical persuasion, can similarly find much to ponder in the processes of criminal law. A convenient and incisive starting point is provided by a recent Law Commission Report (1978) on the mental element in crime. The account of legal matters which follows in the present paper is drawn exclusively from this report, and the paragraph numbers are in reference to the paragraphs of the report only.

In making judgements about *mens rea*, a number of special cases have been recognized, all of them of some specialized interest to psychologists (Para. 4). Firstly, children under the age of 10 are entirely exempt from criminal responsibility, though children between the ages of 10 and 14 may be held criminally liable for an offence if they did the prohibited act knowing that the act was against the law or (surprisingly) knowing that the act was morally wrong. Second, mental disorder or abnormality of the mind may either relieve a defendant of legal responsibility altogether or may lead to a reduction in the seriousness of the offence charged. Third, a defendant will not be found guilty of an offence if it can be shown that there was no 'conscious exercise of the will'. Thus a muscular movement must be voluntary, and it is accepted that a state of 'non-insane automatism' can result from drink or drugs, from physical injury such as concussion, or even from such a natural phenomenon as sleep-walking. Such cases are treated, as are cases of physical coercion, as ones in which the act cannot truly be said to have been committed *by* the defendant.

Naturally, all these situations can give rise to much debate and uncertainty. Psychologists may feel that they have special competence with them, especially of course with respect to those relating to abnormal functioning. Psychologists may also feel they are able to contribute to the discussion about the appropriate disposal of those who have been shown to have committed deeds for which courts, for any of the above reasons, do not hold them responsible. Of more general interest in the present discussion, however, is the vast majority of cases in criminal law for which no extenuating circumstances absolve defendants from being capable of being held responsible for their own actions. The Law Commission Report provides an extensive review of how the criminal law operates in such cases and reveals some interesting uncertainties.

The first uncertainty is to be found in the fact that some crimes appear to be formulated as crimes of strict liability: that is to say their specification makes no reference to a required state of mind. For example, the offence of bigamy is committed by a person who, 'being married, shall marry another person, during the life of the former husband or wife' (Para. 31). Similarly, the Police Act, 1964 provides that 'any person who assaults a constable in the execution of his duty . . . shall be guilty of an offence' (Para. 26). The beliefs or knowledge of a defendant appear to be irrelevant to these offences, and the concept of *mens rea* would seem not to be applicable. However, the Law Commission Report (Para. 30) suggests that the courts generally approach even these statutory offences with an initial presumption in favour of the necessity of a mental element in the offence. They presume in general that Parliament intended the offence to incorporate some element of *mens rea* appropriate to the offence. Thus a person who had good reason to suppose his spouse to be dead might not be found guilty of the offence of bigamy despite the uncompromising wording of the offence itself.

The presumption of a required element of *mens rea* in offences which are apparently specified in terms of strict liability is illustrated in the Law Commission's Report by a number of specific cases (Paras. 31–39). One of these is the well-known case in 1970 of *Sweet v. Parsley*. The defendant was the subtenant of a farmhouse where she let out several rooms and which she visited only occasionally. Cannabis was found at the farm. Although it was conceded that she had no knowledge that cannabis was being smoked at the house, the appellant was charged under the now superseded Dangerous Drugs Act, 1965 with being concerned in the management of premises used for the purpose of smoking cannabis. Although the relevant sub section of the Act is couched in a way that has no reference to a required mental element, the appellant's original conviction was reversed on appeal in the House of Lords. One of the Law Lords argued that 'being concerned in the management of premises used for smoking cannabis' did not mean being concerned in the management of premises as such, on which cannabis had in fact been smoked, but rather connoted a 'purposeful management activity . . . being concerned in the management of . . . a cannabis smoking den or parlour' (Para. 35). Thus by means of the introduction of implied purposefulness, the concept of *mens rea* is introduced to what appears to be an offence of strict liability. In this way, those who innocently let premises are protected from being found liable for offences which are committed on them without their knowledge.

The Law Commission Report also reveals a good deal of uncertainty in the interpretation of Acts in which a mental element is explicitly identified in the formulation of an offence. One of the main problems here centres on the imprecision of the words used to denote mental events. The report (Para. 9) quotes Lord Simon of Glaisdale, who referred to 'chaotic terminology':

Will, volition, motive, purpose, object, view, intention, intent, specific intent or intention, wish, desire; necessity, coercion, compulsion, duress – such terms which do indeed overlap in certain contexts, seem frequently to be used interchangeably, without definition, and regardless that in some cases the legal usage is a term of art differing from the popular usage.

The Law Commission Report reviews some of the difficulties in current law resulting from the imprecision of terms such as 'maliciously', 'wilfully', 'intent', 'knowledge', and 'recklessness' (Paras. 10–24). Such imprecision rests strangely with the traditional precision of legal argument and process. This is illustrated prettily by cases (Para. 9) bought in 1921 and 1936 under the Larceny Act, 1861 (since repealed by the Theft Act, 1968) which created the offence of 'unlawfully and wilfully' killing a house pigeon. In these two cases, defendants who shot and killed a house pigeon and subsequently claimed to have believed that it was a wild pigeon were held to be guilty of the offence. Such a conclusion shows a fine regard for what would today be called the deep structure of language, apparently resting on the interpretation that the defendant did wilfully kill a creature, that that creature was in fact a house pigeon (though wrongly identified as a wild pigeon by the defendant), and that the defendant therefore wilfully killed a house pigeon.

As a result of its review, the Law Commission Report (1978) recommends that the number of words relating to required mental elements in crime be drastically reduced in future legislation. It recommends that only four such terms be used, each carefully defined. In the light of its discussion of strict liability offences, the Commission urges that all future legislation should take pains to specify or omit these four mentalistic words as appropriate. The four concepts are those of 'intention' (Para. 44), 'knowledge' (Para. 49), 'reckless-ness' (Para. 65) and 'negligence' (Para. 67).

In making these recommendations, the Law Commission Report hopes to reduce the scope for differences of interpretation about the specification of criminal offences, and thereby to increase the consistency of legal judgements. However, it is clear that although this tidying-up exercize would serve to reduce the noise surrounding the decisions, the courts would still be faced with the problems of deciding whether the required mental elements of a crime actually did exist within the accused person at the time when he committed the relevant act. This point can be illustrated by the Report's definition of 'inten-tion' (Para. 44): 'a person should be regarded as intending a particular result of his conduct if, but only if, either he actually intends that result or he has no substantial doubt that the conduct will have that result'. The courts must continue to be confronted with the difficult task of deciding whether a defen-dant did 'actually intend' the result of his action or whether he had 'no substantial doubt' that it would occur, and are therefore faced still with the task of deciding whether a person's account of his own mental activities at the time of the offence is to be trusted or believed. This issue is addressed in Part V of the Law Commission's Report (Paras. 92–98).

The legal process has, in fact, shown interesting changes in emphasis from time to time with respect to the primacy of a mental event in committing a crime. One extreme is to be found in the case of *D.P.P. v. Smith* 1961 (Para. 93). Here the House of Lords decided that a jury should be bound to infer an intent to kill or to inflict grievous bodily harm if 'an ordinary reasonable man' in the position of the alleged murderer would have foreseen death or grievous bodily harm as the natural and probable consequence of this act. This case appeared to place rather little emphasis on the actual mental state of the defendant at the time of the offence, since he may correctly deny that he intended the offence at the time (a correctness which only he, of course, is able in principle to verify). Regardless of the existence or non-existence of relevant private events within the defendant, the jury should infer *mens rea* by reference to what a reasonable man would have foreseen in those circumstances. This is not perhaps the place to labour the difficulties inherent in the concept of 'the reasonable man', but it is important here to note that the decision with respect to *Smith* has been superseded by the Criminal Justice Act, 1967. This specifies that a court or jury shall *not* be bound to infer that an accused person intended a result of his actions by reason only of its being a natural and probable consequence of those actions, but shall decide whether he did intend the result by reference to all the evidence (Para. 93), including presumably the accused person's own self-report.

A case which illustrated an extreme emphasis on the primacy of mental elements in crime is the well-published *D.P.P. v. Morgan and Others* 1976 (Para. 95). Here the House of Lords decided with regard to the offence of rape, which involves sexual intercourse with a woman without her consent, that if the defendant genuinely believed that the woman consented to intercourse he is not guilty even though a reasonable man in his positon would have believed that there was no consent. Thus the reasonableness or otherwise of the belief is not relevant to the defence that the man believed that consent was given by the woman (except in so far as the reasonableness of the belief may be important as evidence tending to show whether that belief was actually held by the defendant at the time). This interpretation too has been superseded by subsequent legislation: the Sexual Offences (Amendment) Act, 1976 specifies that a man may be guilty of rape if the woman did not consent to sexual intercourse and at the time he knew she did not consent or he was *reckless* as to whether she consented (Para. 96).

The Law Commission Report concludes that in determining whether a person has committed an offence, courts or juries should refer to all the evidence, drawing such inferences as appear proper (Para. 98). This has to be put alongside their recommendation that criminal offences be specified in terms of a severely restricted set of mental concepts which are employed explicitly in the formulation of offences. For example, where the specification of an offence explicitly requires that a person *intends* a particular result of his conduct or *knows* that a particular circumstance exists, then it is a *relevant* factor to consider the natural and probable consequence of his conduct or whether a reasonable man would have known that those circumstances existed, in addition to the self-report of the accused person as to his mental state at the time of the offence.

The Law Commission Report on the mental element in crime (1978) provides a useful introduction to the way in which criminal law has confronted some of the issues relating to mental events. Of particular interest to psychologists is its emphasis on the multiplicity and vagueness of terms relating to cognitive events within the general precision of criminal law and, of course, its review of the general problem of interpreting whether the mental states specified in an offence existed in a defendant at the time he committed the deed in question, while recognizing that he has unique and privileged access to these events which he may abuse. In practice, this dilemma is resolved by seeking evidence within the circumstances of the putative crime which may be considered in addition to the self-report of the accused person.

Kenny has argued that '[a] legal system which took no account of states of mind would be as chimeric as it would be abhorrent' (1978, p. 93). He is somewhat resistant to what he sees as the determinism of the social sciences in socio-legal studies, believing them to have little place for mind. However, one might readily adapt Kenny's statement by suggesting that a *psychological* system which took no account of states of mind would also be both chimeric and abhorrent. The problem for psychology, perhaps even more than for law, is *how* to incorporate and deal with private events in relation to publicly observable behaviour.

A contemporary approach which has discussed this issue more openly than most is provided by a radical behaviourism or functional analysis, about which Skinner has written a great deal (for example, Skinner, 1969, 1971, 1974). The suggestion that contemporary behaviourism has anything to offer here sometimes gives rise to surprise. Behaviourism is often thought to be a system in psychology which is applicable largely to rats or pigeons, interprets their behaviour within a mechanistic stimulus-response framework, and has no place for events within an organism, even at a physiological level let alone at a cognitive level. I have discussed these misconceptions elsewhere (Blackman, 1980).

Skinner describes radical behaviourism as a philosophical interpretation of the empirical science of behaviour. One major theme in this approach, which is discussed in the context of psychology as a whole in his book *About Behaviorism* (Skinner, 1974), is certainly that behaviour can be understood in a real sense by relating it to the environmental circumstances in which it occurs. Two aspects of the environment are important, the setting conditions in which the behaviour occurs and the environmental consequences of the behaviour in those conditions. The emphasis on the function of environmental events in influencing behaviour does not however commit radical behaviourists to a simple push–pull or stimulus–response model which accords to man the status of a mindless puppet: it merely emphasizes the undoubted relevance of environmental influences on what we do. Thus relationships can be established empirically between certain setting conditions and what we do, and the functional significance of the pay-offs for what we do can also be demonstrated empirically. Radical behaviourists argue that such relationships provide a real but often systematically overlooked *explanation* of behaviour – that it makes scientific (and sometimes practical) sense to assert that a pattern of behaviour occurs *because* of the environmental setting conditions and/or because of the consequences of such behaviour in those conditions in the past.

A glance at Skinner's writings should dispel any belief that radical behaviourism has no place for mental life. For example, Skinner (1974) includes chapters in *About Behaviorism* on topics such as perceiving, thinking and knowing, all of which are cognitive concepts. Skinner therefore in no sense denies the reality of such cognitions for the perceiver, the thinker or the knower. Similarly he does not deny the existence of physiological processes within an organism – how could he? However, he does take the somewhat unusual position of not assigning any *special* causal or explanatory status to events at other levels (cognitive or physiological) in determining behaviour. To do this, he argues, would be to draw the attention of psychologists away from the important relationships between behaviour and the environment which are open to public observation. While physiological events are in principle open to public observation, in practice they must be the domain of skilled physiologists. Cognitive events, on the other hand, can in principle never be directly open to public scrutiny. Despite these limitations, however, there is a tendency for us to accept as 'good' explanations for behaviour accounts which emphasize either unobserved physiological processes or unobservable cognitive events, often when such accounts provide no more than untestable paraphrases of the observable behaviour. Such explanations, Skinner argues, are certainly not inherently better than explanations of behaviour in terms of its observable relationships with environmental circumstances and consequences.

For these reasons, mental or physiological events are not seen by radical behaviourists as somehow autonomous prime movers of behaviour. Instead they are themselves considered as being subject to environmental influences, as is overt behaviour. To say that a person does something because he chooses to do so, for example, can have the effect of providing a spurious explanation of his behaviour which does no more than paraphrase the fact that he behaves in that way and which is not open to empirical test. Moreover, if inner or cognitive events are seen as autonomous, such an explanation can have the stultifying effect of preventing further important questions from being asked about the behaviour, such as what made the person choose to behave in that way. Radical behaviourists would argue that the choice itself can be considered as a function of the consequences of behavioural acts in similar circumstances in the past. Thus cognitions are seen as being constructed by the environmental contingencies to which we are exposed, as is our repertoire of overt behaviour. In this process, verbal behaviour and its interactions with environmental circumstances and consequences plays an important role.

Skinner's paper 'Behaviorism at fifty' with its subsequent addenda (see Skinner, 1969) remains in some ways the clearest account of this view. He makes a distinction between 'seeing', for example, and 'seeing that we see'. It is possible for external observers to judge that I see a particular colour by detecting any patterns of behaviour which occur differentially in the presence of that colour. Thus a correlation can be established between lights of certain physically specified wavelengths and particular patterns of behaviour. Parents, for example, may reward a child or show pleasure if he utters the word 'red' in circumstances which they judge to be appropriate, namely when objects are present which have a colour within a particular range. Their reaction (either deliberately or accidental) may in turn lead to a greater probability that the child will utter the word 'red' again when appropriate circumstances are present. The use of the word in circumstances which are judged to be inappropriate will be followed by different consequences. Thus the child is 'shaped' to behave differentially in the presence of specifiable aspects of the environment, and we may say that the child is able to see red. We cannot of course share the experience of redness which we assume to be perceived by the child. However, if the child *reports* that he *sees* red, we may again look to the environmental circumstances to decide whether such a statement can be regarded as appropriate and should therefore be followed by certain consequences. Skinner argues that we become conscious of redness (we 'see that we see' redness, for example) when certain environmental events impinge on us, producing in us sensations which are by their very nature private (though real) and when the community at the same time tells us that we see ourselves seeing red by its behaviour towards us. Thus the verbal community of which we are members can be said to be making its best efforts to establish the private event prompted by physical stimulation (to which it can of course have no direct access) as the appropriate setting conditions in which the reflexive verbal statement about awareness can be considered appropriate. Although others cannot have direct access to the private event, they can at least use the physical world as some form of check on the authenticity of the statement about an inner experience. Of course, people may claim to 'see' things in unusual circumstances (for example, when their eyes are shut). In such cases, the verbal community may take the report of the experience on trust if they have in the past found such statements to be uttered by the person in appropriate environmental circumstances.

This process becomes more tenuous as external referents become less directly relevant to inner experience. For example, it is sometimes more difficult for parents to find external authentification for a child's claim that he is suffering a pain or feeling unwell. In some cases, the claim may readily be related to observable inflammation of part of the body; in others, however, it may be judged only indirectly by reference to general signs of debility such as lethargy or paleness. In such circumstances, it is not surprising that the language used (and the experiences themselves) become less precise and more diffuse, for there is no objective criterion against which statements relating to malaise can be authenticated or calibrated. In contrast, words relating to the experience of vision can be tagged very closely indeed to specifiable and publicly observable features of the environment. Some important private experiences are far removed from specific environmental tags, as for example experiences of and statements about love, depression or sadness. Here it is more difficult still to find a standard against which the inner experience can be calibrated, the words and the experiences themselves become even more diffuse, and it becomes more and more difficult to be confident that words are being used consistently by different people.

Radical behaviourism, then, does have a place for private experiences such as these. Their existence is not denied, but it is recognized that they are not open to public scrutiny. The position can be summarized by the suggestion that consciousness is a social phenomenon shaped in us with varying degrees of efficiency by the people with whom we interact. Concepts such as choice, intentionality and purposefulness are dealt with in a similar way. Radical behaviourists do not deny that in some situations we may feel that we choose to act in certain ways. However, such choice is not accorded logical priority over behaviour and is not interpreted independently of other variables: we may choose to behave in particular ways as a function of what has happened to us in the past and to that extent are led to our choices, and we may be aware of and discuss the experience of choice as a function of the way in which our verbal community interacts with us when more than one option can be perceived for our behaviour. Intentionality and purposefulness are treated in a similar way. Of course, we often experience such feelings, and they are real for us even if they cannot be observed directly by others. However, our intentions and purposes are not to be regarded as somehow independent of all our past interactions with our environment and therefore somehow special or auto-nomous causes of our behaviour. Nor are our awareness and our verbal report of our intentions and purposes to be regarded in vacuo. Radical behaviourists would suggest that the verbal community of which we are members generates self-descriptive and purposive accounts of behaviour in the way that it gene-rates other forms of consciousness and feelings: we are asked what we are doing and why we are doing it, and the verbal community reacts to our answers in ways which seem appropriate in relation to observable events. If we report our purposes and intentions, others may look for the events which follow our behaviour in question and which may support the assertion of purposiveness. They may then strengthen the future probability of our talking about these observable relationships between behaviour and environment in terms of our purpose and the private experience of purposiveness. The verbal community can therefore be thought of as teaching us that we are conscious and that we are purposeful through its interactions with us. Although consciousness and purposefulness are real if private events, radical behaviourists would conceptualize neither as independent or special explanations of what we do.

This short exposition of aspects of contemporary behaviourism inevitably fails to capture some of the complexity of its analysis of private events or mental elements. In particular, it falsely implies a unidirectional influence in which our verbal community teaches us the rules of experience and self-report; in practice, the verbal community consists of individuals exposed to similar environmental contingencies, and therefore consciousness can be said to result from the functional *interactions* between members of a community rather than from some deliberate or poorly defined programme of teaching (see Blackman, 1980). Nevertheless, it can be seen that radical behaviourism and criminal law have considerable points of contact. Both have been confronted by, and have tried to deal with, the nature of the relationship between cognitive experience and overt behaviour and the problem of interpreting or attributing private events in relation to verbal reports about those events.

Behaviourists' analysis of the language of private experience emphasizes (as do other analyses) that words or concepts may become diffuse when detached from potential external referents. Criminal law has also been confronted by the vagueness of such words, though in recommending a reduction in the number of permissible concepts in future legislation, the Law Commission Report (1978) inevitably sustains a firm base in the commonsense interpretation of those words as reflecting some 'given'. It is interesting to note how courts of law have been prepared to greater or lesser extent to evaluate whether a required mental element in crime existed by reference to the circumstances *in addition* to the self-report of the accused person, for behaviourists have suggested that such evidence is a crucial factor in the establishment of language relating to events which are not themselves open to direct public scrutiny.

Behaviourism and current legal process appear to part company, however, with respect to the emphasis which should be placed on private experience in evaluating what a person does. Contemporary behaviourists certainly do not deny the reality of private events, but suggest that they should not necessarily be seen as autonomous prime causes of behaviour which are somehow unaffected by past experience or other variables. Behaviourists would argue that such events are as much to be evaluated as the products of environmental influences as are the overt actions of an accused person. It is sometimes suggested that the concept of *mens rea* is designed to give effect to the idea of *just* punishment and to protect those who accidentally or inadvertently commit an antisocial deed which they are not likely to do again. Thus the culpability for crime appears to rest within the autonomy of the normally required mental element. However, the analysis of mental events as fundamental as knowing or intending as the end products of a chain of influence (in this case as the result of past experience) raises questions about the very concept of blame. Skinner has argued within his deterministic and environmental analysis that we give a person credit for his achievements to the extent that we can see no other explanation for his behaviour (Skinner, 1971). It could be claimed that the general course of psychology has been to identify further influences on behaviour, and these might be taken as reducing in some ways the credit which should be accorded to a person for his achievements. The argument can be extended to the concept of blame. Perhaps we tend to blame a person for his conduct in relation to our ability to identify any influences on his behaviour. Thus the legal concept of responsibility is affected by influences such as mental illness. A failure to identify such extenuating circumstances leads to a tendency to attribute the behaviour to 'internal' cognitive events and the legal process is to some extent built around these events. However, behaviourist analyses of cognitive events in normal people emphasize that they can be seen as dependent variables rather than as autonomous independent variables which are the prime cause of behaviour. This view of course raises questions about whether it is appropriate to blame a person or hold him legally responsible for his actions *because* of any reported (or inferred) cognitive events, when those events are themselves the natural result of processes shaped in him by his interactions in a verbal community for which he is not solely responsible.

This is not, of course, necessarily to argue for the exoneration of proscribed offences or for the capricious incarceration of the accidental offender. However, the behaviourist's approach does tend to suggest that less emphasis be placed on the articulation of 'guilty' sentiments and more on a direct analysis of what the accused person did, of what the observed circumstances were in which he did it, and of the perceived likelihood of his doing it again if allowed the opportunity to do so. In this latter connection, the verbal report of private experience by a defendant is highly relevant evidence, since of course what a person says is often (but not necessarily) of considerable predictive value with respect to what he does.

Behaviourism would appear, then, to put less emphasis on judgements of the mental elements involved at the time a crime is committed, though it does not deny that some people may have and may be able or willing to report experiences of knowledge or intentionality to which the traditional legal process ascribes culpability. The interpretation of self-reports of cognitive experience at the time of a crime is fraught with practical difficulties attributable to the imprecision of language and the privileged access to the mental events of the accused person, and so courts have proved themselves prepared to judge the existence of *mens rea* when it is consistently denied by the defendant (and, less frequently, to judge the absence of *mens rea* when it is consistently affirmed by a 'false' confession). Perhaps it would be no bad thing in the light of such problems to reduce the emphasis on *mens rea*, while taking steps to prevent capricious sentencing by judging *deeds* rather than minds in relation to all their circumstances.

In this short essay, I have tried to suggest that criminal law and contemporary psychology have at their core similar fundamental questions concerning the relationship between mental life and overt behaviour and how to interpret the mental life of other people. I have chosen to illustrate these problems by reference to one contemporary approach to psychology which I happen to favour, namely that of radical behaviourism. However, these basic issues must be confronted by any systematic approach in psychology. Even this preliminary analysis suggests that the strategies adopted by law for dealing with questions relating to mental life provide a great deal of instructive material for psychologists to consider. The mutual interests of law and psychology are certainly not confined to specific questions of abnormal behaviour, jury behaviour, rules of evidence and the like, but go to the roots of the models of man adopted within the two disciplines and within society as a whole. Criminal law provides perhaps the most well developed account of contemporary common sense in relation to human conduct and has a fund of practical experience against which the achievements and aspirations of any systematic approach to psychology can be evaluated.

References

Blackman, D. E. (1980) Images of man in contemporary behaviourism. In Chapman, A. J. and Jones, D. M. (Eds), *Models of Man*, Leicester: British Psychological Society (pp. 99–112).

Joynson, R. B. (1974) *Psychology and Common Sense*, London: Routledge and Kegan Paul.

Kenny, A. (1978) *Freewill and Responsibility*, London: Routledge and Kegan Paul.

Shotter, J. (1975) *Images of Man in Psychological Research*, London: Methuen.

Skinner, B. F. (1969) *Contingencies of Reinforcement: A Theoretical Analysis*, New York: Appleton-Century-Crofts.

Skinner, B. F. (1971) *Beyond Freedom and Dignity*, New York: Knopf.

Skinner, B. F. (1974) *About Behaviorism*, New York: Knopf.

The Law Commission (1978) *Report on the Mental Element in Crime*, London: HMSO.

Implications for Sentencing of Psychological Developments in Behavioural Assessment and Treatment

D. A. BLACK*

The past two decades have seen a great deal of progress in psychological 'technology'. This happens also to represent the lifetime of the Psychology Department at Broadmoor Hospital which, as I am familiar with it, serves to illustrate the contribution this technology has made and its implications for what could possibly be done in the future where the disposal of offenders is concerned.

Psychological technology is rooted in scientific theory and experimentation. With the aid of a diagram to represent the scientific method (Figure 1) I should like to take you through the stages of our work at Broadmoor to illustrate how a body of knowledge and technology has now been assembled with which to tackle the investigation, description, explanation and 'changing' ('treatment') of offender-patients in particular (but with implications for offenders in general).

Collecting Basic Information and Drawing Inferences from the Trends seen

The initial stage of observation (Figure 1) consisted, at Broadmoor, of the collection of standard data from intelligence tests and personality question-naires and relating the results to the characteristics of patients on arrival in and departure from the hopsital. The annual turnover of patients (about 70 per annum then and now; about 130 per annum at the maximum turnover period of the middle 1960s) made it possible to do this with the entire male popula-tion. The results of intelligence testing were useful individually (for identifying impairment; estimating treatment and educational potentials; making a

---

*Consultant Clinical Psychologist, Broadmoor Hospital, Crowthorne, Berkshire.

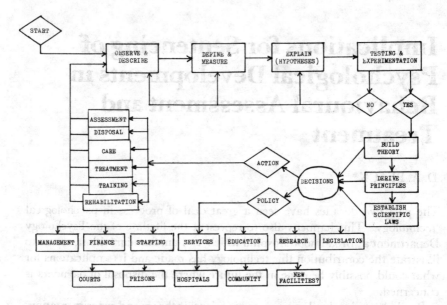

Figure 1. Scientific method as applied to the socio-legal problems of offender behaviour.

placement on discharge) but yielded little that could be said to have policy implications. Personality questionnaires, however, showed interesting patterns in different offender and psychiatric groups. Although those patterns were initially hypothesized to be largely produced by temporary situational factors (such as defensiveness arising from knowledge that discharge from indeterminate hospitalization depends on the achievement of stability and normality) they were later shown by Blackburn (1968) to be more often linked with enduring personality traits. Blackburn's work (1971) enabled a typology of offenders to be described which relates well with both Megargee's (1966) 'extreme' and 'moderate' assaulters dichotomy (Figure 2 and Table 1) and the well-known dimensional structure which most factorial studies of question-naires reveal (Figure 3). The dimensional location of the characteristics of the extreme and moderate assaulters suggests a dimension of control (over-control vs impulsivity in Figure 3) which itself seems to have implications for sen-tencing (or disposal under the 1959 Mental Health Act). The impulsive, 'under-controlled' offender may benefit from a disposal that enables self control to be achieved and which provides alternative 'socialized' solutions for episodes of lost control. The over-controlled offender (whose offences tend to be isolated but more catastrophic) will find a control-producing environment

Table 1. Megargee's extreme and moderate assaulters grouping.

Extreme assault group	Moderate assault group
Attack causing or likely to cause death of a victim	Attack causing or likely to cause pain or injury
Defining offences	
Murder	Occasioning bodily harm
Attempted murder	Wounding with intent to cause grievous
Manslaughter	bodily harm (GBH)
Wounding with intent to murder (WWI)	Wounding with intent to cause actual
	bodily harm (ABH)
	Malicious wounding
	Unlawful wounding
	Assault
Hypotheses confirmed	
(a) Previous history	
Less incidence of previous convictions	Usually many past convictions
(b) Victim	
Usually well known or member of family	Usually stranger or casual acquaintance
(c) Psychological measures	

Less	Impulsivity	More
More	Controls	Less
More	Repression	Less
Introverted	Intro/extraversion	Extraverted
Less	Hostile attitudes	More
More	Denial	Less
More	Social conformity	Less

Neuroticism/anxiety not differentiated

counter-productive (though usually thriving in it as a model patient or prisoner). This does nothing for him, however, where learning to recognize and express emotional conflict is concerned. Instead his disposal requires a setting where traditional psychotherapy, social skills training and the more expressive, possibly 'encounter group' type of treatment ('change producing strategy') are available.

Already, therefore, in terms of the scientific method diagram (Figure 1) we have moved from observation to collation, organization and explanation. We have also encountered hypothesis testing in the Blackburn replication of Megargee's work which resulted in the rejection of the situational hypothesis

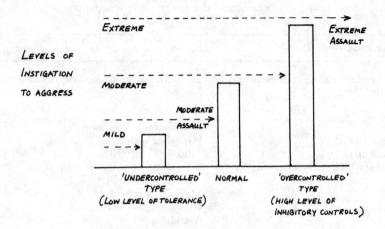

Figure 2. Impulse control types.

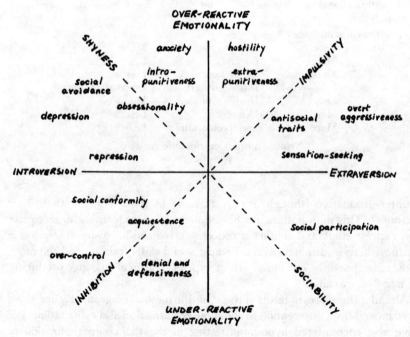

Figure 3. Personality dimensions from questionnaires.

(explanation) of defensiveness envisaged originally and described above. We have also moved on to a suggestion for a practical application of the findings which itself is a further hypothesis (which should be tested in a practical situation) but at least has the merit of being based on systematic observation and theory rather than untested opinions or merely the prevailing social climate of retributive justice.

Investigating the Specific Determinants of Abnormal Traits

At around the end of the first decade of psychological work at Broadmoor our work was at the stage of, as it were, categorizing the main coping strategies which people used to deal with problems and stresses in life. The work had suggested that in cases of mental disorder either:

(1)   strategies for coping with stress are impaired by misperceptions, thought disorder, inappropriate emotional warning signals etc.; or

(2)   the degree of perceived stress, which acts as the provocation or instigation to aggress, is greatly magnified by the hallucinatory perceptions, deluded interpretations or over-reactive emotional responses of the individual who 'suffers' from or presents these disorders.

Individual Perceptions of Stress

The next step became that of identifying the particular stresses, internally perceived or externally present, to which a particular individual is vulnerable. Identifying a personality trait (that is, a tendency to use a particular coping strategy more often than others) does not indicate the context in which the use of the strategy will occur. Conversely, identifying the particular vulnerability or sensitivity of an individual does not indicate the strategy he will employ to solve, avoid or eliminate the problem. With both sets of information – not only *how* the individual tends to respond, but also *what* perceived problem he is responding to, see Figure 4 – we may be getting nearer to seeing the whole picture.

During the second decade at Broadmoor (the 1970s) two work trends looked more closely into methods of making up the second component in this equation — the contextual or individual vulnerability component.

(i) Cognitive approach. The first of these two trends is the work of Howells (1976, 1978), set in the context of attribution theory, and using amongst other things the 'repertory grid' technique to identify an individual's construing of his personal world – the people and situations within it and their inter-relation-

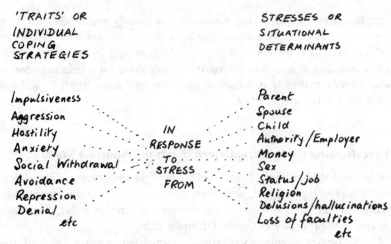

Figure 4. Example of individual–situation interaction possibilities.

ships and perceived threat. Figure 5 illustrates a 'persons' grid whilst Figure 6 illustrates a 'situations' grid. A grid is thus essentially a questionnaire where a set of questions (elements) are all answered in terms, not of yes or no or true or false but of a set of values or criteria (constructs). If all the elements and constructs are elicited from the patient rather than supplied by the researcher, then a projective element is incorporated. Usually a combination of elicited and supplied elements and constructs is used. The squares in the girid may be scored simply as 'present' or 'absent' (1 or 0) or ranked or rated and each method has its merits according to the situation. By this method Howells showed that it was possible to identify feelings associated with certain people or situations and actions associated with feelings, thus supplying context to personal traits as well as elaborating on the variety of traits which might occur in different situations and which would not necessarily be revealed by the cruder questionnaire method. For instance Howells (1977) was able to confirm the often expressed view that rape is committed for a variety of reasons and not only or even principally for sexual gratification. Hostility and the desire to humiliate is a frequent motive.

(ii) Physiological approach. The second work trend at this stage is set in the area of measurement of physiological changes associated with psychological events and is exemplified by the work of Hinton in the first half of the 1970s and Crawford latterly. This approach again is relevant to the second or contextual component of the explanation of the individual's behaviour. Arousal of the autonomic nervous system, associated with perceived emotional stress or pleasure, may be monitored in various ways, such as changes in breathing or

Figure 5

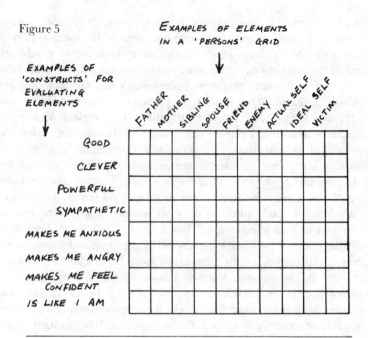

Examples of elements in a 'Persons' grid

Examples of 'constructs' for evaluating elements

Elements: FATHER, MOTHER, SIBLING, SPOUSE, FRIEND, ENEMY, ACTUAL SELF, IDEAL SELF, VICTIM

Constructs: GOOD, CLEVER, POWERFUL, SYMPATHETIC, MAKES ME ANXIOUS, MAKES ME ANGRY, MAKES ME FEEL CONFIDENT, IS LIKE I AM

Figure 6

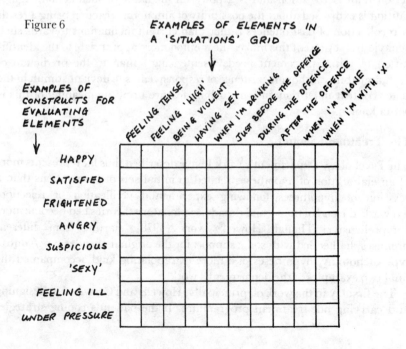

Examples of elements in a 'Situations' grid

Examples of constructs for evaluating elements

Elements: FEELING TENSE, FEELING 'HIGH', BEING VIOLENT, HAVING SEX, WHEN I'M DRINKING, JUST BEFORE THE OFFENCE, DURING THE OFFENCE, AFTER THE OFFENCE, WHEN I'M ALONE, WHEN I'M WITH 'X'

Constructs: HAPPY, SATISFIED, FRIGHTENED, ANGRY, SUSPICIOUS, 'SEXY', FEELING ILL, UNDER PRESSURE pulse rates, in electrical conductivity of the skin, in muscle tension, in pupil diameter and, in sexual contexts, in penile tumescence. Hinton and O'Neill (1978) have described differences in the orienting responses of psychiatric groups and in the recovery curves of some response categories. The arousing stimuli were visual or sound pictures of pleasant or distressing scenes and cognitive tasks, and also tactile shock (cold pressor). Woodman, Hinton and O'Neill (1978) have also found interesting biochemical differences (adrenaline/noradrenaline balance) associated with offender categories ('domestic' vs 'public' offenders – a dichotomy rather similar to Megargee's and Blackburn's extreme and moderate assaulters or over- and under-controlled personality types). Crawford's work (1979) has included monitoring of penile response to a variety of videotaped sequences of sexual activity, adult-adult and adult-child; male-female, male-male, female-female; and violent and affectionate. Thus he has been able to describe in individuals the contexts which are most sexually arousing and which, in the case of abnormal practices, might constitute a social hazard in the future or a treatment need in the present. Caution has to be adopted in translating laboratory reactions to real life but the attraction of physiological arousal as an indicator potentially more valid than cognitive responses, especially where involuntary responses are concerned, is that such arousal is both a stage nearer action than is cognition and is a powerful mediator of such action. Again, caution is expressed about the possibility of autonomic reaction being a result of recollection of past offences rather than current inclinations towards such behaviour. At present this makes the method more appropriate to the identification of initial placement needs ('sentencing') than to the prediction of dischargeability although existence of responsiveness to deviant stimuli in the latter context must remain a disturbing feature until the meaning of this is better known.

The Treatment Sequel

The Psychology Department's work I have described thus far represents more of an elaboration of hypotheses related to initial sets of observations than a revision of hypotheses following experimental verification or rejection. Towards the end of the second decade, explanatory theories had become more comprehensive. Though Howell's work (1978), starting from different premises, had ended with some support for the original offender type/control type dichotomy, hypotheses of a more extrapolating kind accompanied the final two examples of the department's work.

The first lay in the work of, principally, Howells and Crawford in designing and carrying out treatment programmes. If the patient's coping strategies were inappropriate then changing these so that personal satisfaction was preserved or increased, while an offending outcome was made less likely, should lend validating support to the coping strategy or trait explanation for the initial offending behaviour. If vulnerable or sensitive areas could be rendered less so by desensitization, or resensitization to an alternative stimulus source, and if again personal satisfaction was preserved and offending decreased, then once more the validity of the explanation would be enhanced.

Howells' work developing social skills training for socially withdrawn (and even inept) young men certainly seems to have effected significant improvement of social functioning and of personal satisfaction in many cases. Crawford's (1979) programmes have become more comprehensive in combining social skills training with such other approaches as relaxation training, positive reconditioning and sex education programmes. (He has focussed on sex offenders, many of whom combine lack of socially appropriate behaviours with anxiety in the presence of the opposite sex, arousal to inappropriate sexual stimuli and ignorance of basic sexual information.) Again it is possible to point to improved social functioning, normal responding in the laboratory and improved sexual knowledge, together with greater subjectively expressed personal satisfaction. As to reduced reoffending this has yet to be ascertained. Stays in Broadmoor tend to be long and sizeable discharge samples are slow to accumulate.

Table 2. General description of sample in discharge follow-up study.

Number discharged (males only)	128
During the period	1960–1965 inclusive
Follow-up period	5 years
Follow-up information from	Hospital records
	Special Hospitals Research Unit records
	Mental Health Register
Average age of sample on discharge	41.54 years
Average length of stay	7.48 years
With previous convictions	77 (60 per cent)
With previous psychiatric admissions	63 (49 per cent)
Admitting offence	
Homicide	62 (48 per cent)
Other personal Violence	33 (26 per cent)
Property damage	6 (5 per cent)
Property acquisitive	23 (18 per cent)
Sexual	4 (3 per cent)
Victim	
Wife/partner, etc.	32 (25 per cent)
Other family or well known	44 (34 per cent)
Casual or stranger	20 (16 per cent)

Table 3. Sucess tendencies in discharge follow-up study.

No previous 'history' (offending or psychiatric)
Current offence homicide
Older
Been in Broadmoor longer
Diagnosis 'affective disorder'
Under indeterminate 'sentence' (hospital order now)
Victim family or well known

On psychological assessment prior to discharge:
Less emotional disturbance
More social conformity and control
Some uncertainty with non-verbal problem-solving tasks

Table 4. Failure tendencies in discharge follow-up study.

With previous convictions
Currently property offender or non-homicidal violence
Younger
Been in Broadmoor shorter time
Classified as 'psychopathic disorder'
Under fixed sentence (Section 72 of Mental Health Act now)
Victim stranger or casual acquaintance

On psychological assessment prior to discharge:
(a)   psychiatric re-admissions
more thinking and sensory disturbance ('psychotic')
more hostile attitudes
(b)   re-offenders in general
more impulsive and extraverted ('psychopathic')
(c)   subsequently committed assaults
more impulsive *and* emotionally disturbed

The Discharge Follow-up Sequel

Nevertheless the second example of this latest phase was of a discharge follow-up study carried out by Black (1976). The composition of the sample studied and the main results are summarized in Tables 2, 3 and 4. This was only able to look at success or failure of outcome in relation to a range of basic social, criminological, psychiatric and psychological data already available or obtained on discharge and did not include data on treatment undergone. The sample was in any event one comprising discharges from 1960 to 1965 inclusive when psychological treatment programmes were minimal and most treatments were the conventional psychiatric ones together with the long stay hospital's combination of educational, occupational and recreational programmes. It would have been difficult to distinguish specifically different treatment programmes in a group such as that. What did emerge from my study was strong corroboration for the viability of the dichotomy revealed in previous people's work (Megargee, 1966; Blackburn, 1968; Hinton and O'Neill, 1978; and to some extent Howells 1976, 1978), namely the over-control/undercontrol, domestic/public offender, extreme/moderate assaulter concepts. The summary of success characteristics (Table 3) and failure characteristics (Table 4) look very similar to those in Table 1 with success being markedly greater in the overcontrolled, domestic offender, extreme assaulter group.

Sentencing Implications

These then are some of the psychological developments at Broadmoor over two decades. The implications for sentencing are of two kinds. Firstly, that psychologists have relevant evidence to contribute which is independent of other specialists and which should not, for instance, be included with medical or psychiatric evidence. The psychologist, in the case of criminal violence, can indicate the basic behavioural strategy which typifies the offender; should often be able also to identify the individual causes of that particular offence and should be able to indicate the likelihood of effecting some behavioural change and the setting required to do this. This might be referred to as an 'action' implication. Second, however – and because such actions may not be readily feasible in current conditions (treatment settings are limited) – there are the 'policy' implications. Individual personality characteristics, like environmental circumstances, vary widely. Many of them are normally distributed, statistically, like height and weight, so that it is not possible to draw dividing lines between 'clever', 'average' and 'dull'; or 'emotionally stable and unstable'; or 'in-control-of-impulses' and 'unable-to-control-impulses', any more than it is possible to draw the line between 'tall' and 'short'. These are all relative concepts where extremes may be obvious but elsewhere one quality shades gradually into another. The court's task of deciding between, for instance, 'mad' and 'sane', 'responsible' and 'not responsible' and hence 'guilty' or 'not guilty' is therefore not one which readily lends itself to psychological answers (British Psychological Society, 1973). The 'mad–sane' choice

has been resolved somewhat by the introduction of the diminished responsibility concept but even so the range of choices for subsequent disposal of the
'partly-mad' or the 'not-quite-sane' is very limited and any disposal that is not
to a penal establishment tends to be popularly criticized as a 'let-off'. To
reconcile this seemingly incompatible requirement of the court process and the
nature of psychological phenomena one possibility is that some adaptation of
court procedure might be contemplated. If the court were to separate *actus reus*
from *mens rea* then the court's requirement of first establishing guilt in terms of
'Did he actually do it?' could be satisfied with its attendant consideration of
evidence to satisfy the court. *Mens rea*, or intent, could then be considered in
terms of realistic psychological criteria in order to establish the most appropriate disposal. Psychological evidence deriving from the kind of developments represented by the work at Broadmoor could then be expected to make
comments such as 'Why did he do it?', 'Can he be changed or his problems be
brought under control?'. Comments such as these were put before the Butler
Committee (1975) by the British Psychological Society in their evidence to
that Committee (British Psychological Society, 1973), but the propositions
seemingly received little support at the stage of oral evidence. Since then more
criticism has been levelled at places which detain offenders under indeterminate sentences or hospital orders such as to make it prohibitively difficult to
discharge such offenders. Re-offending is not tolerated in such cases, although
a higher incidence of re-offending is tolerated in prisoners who leave prison at
the expiry of their sentence. A two-part court process separating *actus reus* from
mens rea could be adapted to overcome the discharge problem of the indefinitely
detained offender and is in fact favoured by some criminologists. Thus at the
actus reus stage, if proof is accepted, the 'tariff' penalty could be established. At
the *mens rea* stage appropriate disposal would be decided. If the object of the
disposal was not achieved by the time of expiry of the 'tariff' penalty then the
offender (or patient) would become the responsibility of the appropriate care
facility until the disposal recommendation was complete (or the usual hospital
or local authority procedures had been completed). If the object of the disposal
were achieved *before* expiry of the 'tariff' penalty then a procedure akin to a
Mental Health Review Tribunal, Aarvold Review Board, or Parole Board
could be used, or, preferably a further court procedure, as in some other
countries and states of the USA, which would enable a case for an appropriate
alternative to be examined and argued.

   In fact, the final report of the Butler Committee did suggest amendments to
the law, many of which would achieve, or nearly achieve, the results which are
now proposed as following from psychological practice and research in a
setting such as Broadmoor. Examples are (with my comments on what they

might achieve):

(1)   The two-part 'special verdict' – in effect separating *actus reus* from *mens rea*.

(2)   Remands to hospital – enabling the sort of investigation to be undertaken which could assist disposal.

(3)   Reviewable sentence – to overcome the inability to predict how long is needed to effect a 'treatment' programme.

(4)   Interim hospital orders – allowing disposal destinations to be changed.

(5)   Training units in prisons for psychopaths – to enable 'change' programmes to be implemented for people essentially not a hospital problem.

(6)   Regional secure hospital units – could go some way to fill the gap between prison, secure hospital and open hospital which is needed to facilitate flexible care and 'change' programmes. However, they are not planned to be 'half-way houses' and in some ways preserve the dichotomy rather than providing a continuum of care facility.

Next, of course, there are policy implications from our work in terms of facilities which need developing to cater for any changed court sentencing procedure. Examples are:

(1)   Development of community care and supervision facilities in terms of both bricks and mortar and personnel, for example greater use of Guardianship as well as Probation Orders by a variety of professionals as well as probation officers. This within a service structure allowing greater flexibility of its use and transfer between health services, social services and local authority services.

(2)   Provison for day centre attendance of those needing protective and supportive care and/or the converse: sheltered or supportive work facilities for those residing in institutions or other residential units.

(3)   The growth or adaptation of residential units which fill the gap between hospital and penal establishments. Thus these would be neither for the provision of medical care nor to satisfy a punishment concept. They would instead operate a principle of growth and development towards coping and adaptation to individual circumstances, using professional help of the training kind exemplified by the kind of assessment and treatment developments I have described.

Summary

Psychological developments in the last two decades have been reviewed with reference to clinical and research programmes at Broadmoor Hospital. These have been reviewed in the context of the scientific method to illustrate that developments both need validating and are capable of revision and extension.

From descriptive studies there has grown a typology of behavioural styles, personality traits or coping strategies that enable these to be identified. However, contextual specification of the pressures and stresses to which an individual is susceptible is also required and has been researched by verbal and physiological methods. Some cross-validation of findings has been achieved by treatment and follow-up studies which also add to the ability to specify disposal needs when sentencing.

Implications from this work are of an 'action' and a 'policy' type, the former largely comprising fuller advice to the court on explanations and hence remedial needs for the offender before the court. Implications of a policy type also follow, however, from both the work described and the 'action' implications. Not only are the latter difficult to carry out without legislative or at least procedural changes, but the implications of the work itself are that:

(1) court procedures are ill-suited to the controlling and changing of the mechanisms of offending, explained psychologically; and
(2) the organization of the disposal services is also ill-fitted to cope with the care and change needs of many kinds of violent offender.

Changes in the administrative organization of some existing facilities would help meet the implications of this work whilst changes suggested by the Butler Committee would also go a long way to meeting needs. It is to be hoped that, in the review of the 1959 Mental Health Act, begun by the previous government but not so far announced as part of the present government's programme, there will be attention paid both to the Butler Committee's helpful recommendations and to other needs indicated from recent and current advances in the technologies of applied science.

Acknowledgement and disclaimer

I am grateful to DHSS and Broadmoor Hospital for facilities to enable this work to be carried out but responsibility for opinions expressed is my own.

References

Black, D. A. (1976), 'A five year follow-up study of male patients discharged from Broadmoor Hospital', paper presented to the NATO Advanced Study Institute, Cambridge, July 1976, available in cyclostyle from author and to appear in Gunn, J. and Farrington, D. P. (eds), *Advances in Forensic Psychiatry and Psychology*, John Wiley, Chichester.
Blackburn, R. (1968), 'Personality in relation to extreme aggression in psychiatric offenders', *British Journal of Psychiatry*, **114**, 821–828.

Blackburn, R. (1971), 'Personality types among abnormal homicides', *British Journal of Criminology*, **11**, 14–31.

British Psychological Society (1973), 'Memorandum of evidence to the Butler Committee on the law relating to the Mentally Abnormal Offender', *Bulletin of the British Psychological Society*, **26**, 331–342.

Committee on Mentally Abnormal Offenders (1975), *Report*, Cmnd 6244, (The 'Butler' Report), HMSO, London.

Crawford, D. A. (1979), 'Modification of deviant sexual behaviour: the need for a comprehensive approach', *British Journal of Medical Psychology*, **52**, 151–156.

Hinton, J. W. and O'Neill, M. T. (1978), 'Pilot research on psychophysiological response profiles of maximum security hospital patients', *British Journal of Social and Clinical Psychology*, **17**, 103.

Howells, K. (1976), 'Interpersonal aggression', *International Journal of Criminology and Penology*, **4**, 319–330.

Howells, K. (1977), 'The emotional mediation of sexual offences', paper presented at the British Psychological Society Annual Conference, Exeter, April 1977.

Howells, K. (1978), 'The perception of social causality in "mentally abnormal" aggressive offenders', unpublished PhD thesis, University of Birmingham.

Howells, K. and Wright, E. (1978), 'The sexual attitudes of aggressive sexual offenders', *British Journal of Criminology*, **18**, 2, 170–174.

Megargee, E. I. (1966), 'Undercontrolled and overcontrolled personality types in extreme antisocial aggression', *Psychology Monographs*, **80**, No. 611.

Woodman, D. D., Hinton, J. W. and O'Neill, M. T. (1978), 'Plasma catecholamines and aggression in maximum security patients', *Biological Psychology*, **6**, 147–154.

Pre-trial Publicity

DENNIS HOWITT*

The title of this paper is rather more limited than its substance, since the issues of pre-trial publicity stretch widely through the relationship of the press and mass media in general with the courts. The issue though is largely the basic one of whether or not the news media may in some way alter the course of justice. In other words, the influence of news reports prior to, during, and (even) after a trial on the verdict in a court of law. Even this is rather too limited since the activities of the press need not necessarily appear in news reports to have an influence on the course of justice. For example, the payment for exclusive rights to the publication of the witness's own story has been argued by some as potentially a source of injustice. Of course, the issues that are under discussion here relate closely to the law of contempt of court. Only part of this law is relevant to the news media and pre-trial publicity but the law on contempt covers and governs the media's treatment of court related news to a large extent. It would be wrong however, to reserve our discussion solely and exclusively to issues which are directly relevant to the news media and contempt of court, since contempt has not been applied to many issues which are potentially important in the relationship between the news media and the courts. I will discuss these where I feel appropriate. The paper is in three sections: a general introduction on the news media and the courts; a discussion of research evidence on prejudice; and a brief conclusion.

The News Media and the Courts

In many ways the relationship between the news media and the courts is much less problematic in Britain than in some other countries – the reason being, of course, that we do not have a constitution which guarantees both a free press and a free trial. It is also not really that much of an issue in Britain because, by

*Department of Social Sciences, Longhborough University.

and large, we have few notable instances of direct confrontation between the news media and the courts. Now this is not to ignore the important exceptions which have occurred in recent years but simply a note of the fact that the press has tended to play it very safe in its relations with the courts. The law on contempt is notoriously imprecise and precedents have only a very limited applicability so the media do not have much of a real guideline from which to work. Given this and the facts that the law of contempt enables summary sentences of unlimited fines and imprisonment in Superior Courts – and until 1960 not even the possibility of appeal – it is not surprising that the news media have responded conservatively. Furthermore it is noteworthy that there have been no trials before a *jury* for contempt of court *this century*. Thus in many ways this is referral to public opinion has been excluded in favour of the decisions of the judiciary alone.

The law on contempt in relation to possible prejudicial publications has thus been little tested. The essential principle underlying the application of contempt to the news media seems to be that certain sorts of news stories may prejudice the outcome of a trial. The implicit reason why the news media are assumed to have this power is not too clear but a few quotations of disarming frankness might help reveal something (Committee on Contempt of Court, 1975):

1.   It would, we think, be going much too far to say that professional judges are never influenced by what they may read or hear, but they are by their training and experience capable of putting extraneous matter out of their minds. A judge, therefore, does not need the law of contempt to protect him from prejudicial matter, although wholly unrestricted comment immediately before and during a hearing could be embarrassing, and might constrain him to demonstrate in some manner that he had not been influenced by it. (p. 22).
2.   Much of the law of criminal evidence is based on the assumption that juries are more open to prejudice than professional lawyers in taking account only of strictly relevant matters. (p. 23).
3.   . . . I would not have any contempt . . . Certainly never in a judge-alone case. [Lord Salmon] (p. 98).

So there we have it. We need to control the press for reason of the frailty of the jury – the ease with which they are influenced. I find all this fascinating in that it exactly parallels practically every fear of the adverse effects of the mass media on the audience – whether it be the effects of television violence on children, advertizing, election broadcasting, or pornography. The view is, commonly, that there is a class of people incapable of withstanding the onslaught of the media while at the same time there is another class of people who are totally incorruptible by what the mass media choose to put over

(Howitt and Cumberbatch, 1975). I do not know if there is any evidence at all for the view that the judiciary is robust in contrast with the juror's frailty but clearly there are some legal procedures, like the appeals procedures, which are built, in part, on this assumption.

There are many problems with the law on contempt but one of the most intractable is the temporal dimension within which it operates. For example, if a newspaper publishes, after the charging of a suspect, evidence about a crime which has not been tried, that newspaper may well be in contempt of court. It seems clearly accepted in England and Wales that a criminal charge is the first marker in the judicial process with which the news media may not interfere. In Scotland, this marker seems to have been potentially shifted to an earlier stage by the statement arising out of events in 1960. The Lord Justice General said:

Once a crime has been suspected, and once the criminal authorities are investigating it, they and they alone have the duty of carrying out that investigation. If a newspaper arranges an interview with any person in any way involved with the suspected crime and then publishes the results of the interview, or an article based upon it, the newspaper is doing something which in all probability will interfere with the course of justice and hinder a fair trial. (Committee on Contempt of Court, 1975, p. 11).

This tougher criteron has not yet been tested, but does illustrate the problem of where to draw the line. We should note that this definition, extreme as it might appear, probably excludes prejudicial publicity before a crime is known to the police. But it would be naive to believe that possible prejudice does not exist before this. For example, it is common that accounts of on-going frauds are described in the news media. There are may pieces of investigative journalism which expose crimes well before there is any police involvement. These reports will include tape-recorded evidence, pictures, hearsay evidence, and other forms of proof not necessarily acceptable in courts of law. Witnesses and victims will be interviewed and the offender photographed and even on occasion interviewed himself. Perhaps the offender may add injury to injury by manhandling the reporter. There would seem to be no question but that such reporting does create an impression of guilt in the minds of the viewer and it really does prejudice any later trial in the sense that the word 'prejudice' is commonly used. However, no one has really questioned the media's right to do this except in cases like the South African Government's initial legalistic response to the Muldergate scandal. Clearly it has to be accepted that the news media may have some role in justice. The matter seems to be one of balance but the point of balance has not been too clearly defined. It is difficult, given that we accept that the press has a positive role to play in this matter, to see that it necessarily has to end at the point of charging the suspect. Another element in the temporal dimension of the law of contempt is that although it is not acceptable to publish material which relates to previous convictions during a trial, sometimes, by accident of fate, circumstances contrive to make it impossible not to do so. For example, the Krays had been tried and convicted on one set of charges which were duly publicized in the news media but shortly afterwards were tried on a separate set of charges. It is unlikely that the jurors in the second trial were unaware of the results of the first trial. As clearly as in any other case the Krays were prejudiced by the publicity given the first trial. But, of course, the news media were not charged with being in contempt of court. It seems that the need for a free flow of information becomes paramount in these circumstances, possibly because it is felt that the risk of prejudice is very slight. A further temporal aspect is introduced by the requirement that the reporting of a trial is dealt with contemporaneously.

During the course of the trial, following the charge, the only publicity which may without question be published is what we might term a fair and accurate account of the court proceedings. To anyone with some knowledge of the workings of the mass media such a phrase and such a situation rings a familiar warning bell. This is because underlying it is the assumption that the way in which the mass media may influence the course of justice is by printing damaging information which has not yet been, or will not be, presented in court. But the mass media are capable of a rather different sort of process which might have some quite considerable influence on the jurors. The mass media are by their very nature selective, but they are also constructivist in the sense that they create reality. It is literally impossible for the mass media to present all the court news, never mind all the news that there is. In any case what is news is largely defined by the mass media themselves which further reinforces the description of constructivists.

With this sort of notion in mind we can ask ourselves whether or not it is possible for the news media to make an independent contribution to the course of justice without in any way contravening the law on contempt. The news media inevitably are, as we have said, very selective in what they present. Mass communications researchers have pointed out that the news that we read, see, and hear in the mass media is the product of selection, editing, and even recruitment of materials. The press treatment of a court case is bound to be, at best, a pale imitation of what actually goes on in court. The news values of journalists will tend towards the selection of the most sensational and personifiable aspects of a hearing. Could it not be that this selection of vital aspects of the proceedings might feed back to the jurors? For example, if it is reported out of many things that have been said in court only that Jeremy Thorpe's counsel admits that Thorpe has homosexual tendencies, despite

Thorpe previously denying this, then it may be elevated to a greater importance than it might otherwise warrant in the minds of the jury. We might note in this connection the great variability in the amount reported in the news media about the Thorpe trial from day to day despite in all probability the daily hearings being roughly of equal length. With the demise of the 'juicy bits' the interest of the press grew less. There is no direct evidence which suggests that the selectivity of the press influences the jury, but it does have broad parallels in what is called the 'agenda setting function' of the mass media where there is more support. The phrase 'agenda setting function' designates the tendency of people to accept what the mass media present as the major issues of the day whether or not they accept the media's viewpoint on these. It could be that the media defines as a key issue the fact that Thorpe's homosexual tendencies are now admitted whereas they had previously been denied. This in its turn might lead to the view that the testimony of those claiming, amongst other things, that Thorpe was homosexual was in general much more credible.

Another way in which the media might prejudice justice has, in its general form, received considerable discussion in the literature on the mass media. This is through the process of creating 'moral panics'. By moral panic we mean, for instance, that the media may create an impression that 'muggings' are becoming part of our everyday life, encourage the view that they are more widespread than they in fact are, create a hue and cry that something has to be done about 'muggers', and consequently the 'mugger' when he comes before the court has a much rougher time than he otherwise might. Although it is difficult to get evidence once again of a direct nature there are a number of case studies which suggest this possibility strongly (Chibnall, 1977).

The question of the payment of witnesses for the publication rights of 'their story' contingent on the 'successful' completion of the hearing is a current version, albeit with somewhat different implications, of the older controversy about the payment of criminals for their stories. The older version was ethically much simpler and is based on the premise that it is wrong that criminals grow fat on the proceeds (even indirect ones) of their misdoings. The older version is also simpler in the sense that there is no implication that the criminal is in someway compromised, and justice (of a formal kind) prejudiced by such payments. However, much as one might be inclined to criticize some of the activities of the press in this regard, it is very strange that there seems to have been no attempt to deal with the matter under the laws of contempt though perhaps the reason for this may be very simple since the financial arrangements may be made before a charge has been put. In any case, it is difficult to understand why we should assume that a person will tell the truth if he is going to get £25,000 and lie if he is going to get £50,000 since £25,000 is probably well worth lying for if you are of that sort of inclination. Furthermore, it is naive to believe that witnesses in particularly notorious cases are unaware that the possibilities of rewards would be greatly increased by a conviction whether or not they had entered into any contract before a verdict has been reached. A person who understands that this information has some market value and attempts to exploit it well before the police are involved, might be expected to realise that its worth will accummulate with a conviction. The question also needs to be asked of whether the press's payments to witnesses may encourage witnesses to come forward when otherwise they might not. This is parallel perhaps to the reward system which offers payment for information leading to conviction. We might put the issue more broadly as the question of whether or not investigative journalism has any worthwhile role to play. It is too easy to vilify the press by taking a myopic look at the issues.

In many ways the criticisms of the press assume that the process of law is one of unfettered fairness. To the extent that it is not there exists the possibility, if not the likelihood, that the press might have some role to play in correcting the balance. Fairness is a relative concept and there is some reason to believe that, for example, the police have a much more manipulative role in pre-trial publicity than some might expect. Mass communications researchers use the concept 'news management' which I think is a very powerful and illustrative phrase for a fairly complex social process (for example, Chibnall, 1977). News, as we have said, does not just happen, sometimes it is sought by the news media but sometimes it is given to the media. Like the army in Northern Ireland, government ministers, and many others, the police are in a position to give valuable information to the news media. Sometimes it is given because it suits their purposes, sometimes as part of a process of controlling the press. Sometimes, of course, the police will not give information when it suits their purpose. This is all part of the process of news management – that is, control over the reporting activities of the news media. The following passages taken from Peter Hain's (1976) account of his arrest on the charge of bank robbery is probably as graphic an illustration as we are likely to find:

We had agreed with Wandsworth police not to release news of my detention and charge until after the identity parade on Monday. It is unusual for someone to be charged before an ID parade, and even more unusual for it to be held three days afterwards. In view of the fact that I was publicly known, both the police and my solicitor were anxious that there should be no publicity before the parade. Otherwise it might be invalid.

But could the police be trusted to keep this agreement? Indeed, the *Daily Mirror* acting on a police tip-off, had rung my parents several times while I was still in detention and before I was charged. Only my parents' steadfast refusal to confirm the story prevented the paper carrying it. Even with the police officially refusing to release or confirm the charge, it was highly likely that a police officer somewhere would *unofficially* release it to a Fleet Street contact, and perhaps make himself some pocket money in the process. (p. 19)

In the end, according to Hain, it was Scotland Yard that released the information to the press before the identification parade. Of course, this resulted in a welter of publicity some of which was partly due to the efforts of Hain himself. Some of the publicity Hain describes as treading a very thin line between the *sub judice* rules. It allowed for appeals to witnesses and also for Hain publicly to deny involvement. The response of the news media broadly favoured Hain and was one way that the balance was partially redressed, but was probably only feasible because he was an established public figure. Hain appears to have benefited psychologically from this. In some ways the behaviour of the police in this case contrasts markedly with police treatment of the Neville Heath sex murders 30 years earlier where after the first murder the police prevented the publication of his photograph on the grounds of prejudicing identification evidence – thus, some have argued, allowing him to kill again before being arrested.

We could apply this same concept of news management to a rather different state of affairs – one which is more directly related to the legal profession than the previous example. The ideas inherent in contempt of court and *sub judice* rules are inevitably meant to be mechanisms of social control. Perhaps the phrase 'social control' is much too 'high-falutin' to use in the context of the use of legal processes to prevent public discussion of important issues. 'Gagging writs', which are essentially devices intended to stifle public comment without any real intention of taking the matter to court are graphic examples of this. While such writs tend not to be too successful we have more extreme examples. A classic case, and perhaps the most notorious example, is the *Sunday Times/* Thalidomide affair. The legal problems involved in seeking recompense for the gross deformities suffered by many of the children cannot concern us at the moment, it is the events of 1972 which are more immediately pertinent. The drug Thalidomide had been on the market between 1959 and 1961 and over the years that followed a number of claims had been settled out of court. However, some parents would not or could not settle in this way and litigation was continuing. The *Sunday Times* had begun to publish a series of articles on, amongst other things, the difficulties of the children, when the company, essentially via the Attorney-General, applied for an injunction on the grounds that their case was being prejudiced. The divisional court agreed, the court of appeal disagreed, and the House of Lords agreed. The major difficulty in all of this is not simply that the rules of contempt may operate as a gag – they are designed to do that – but the gag extends to the discussion of important issues which are possibly only minimally related to the case itself. The issue of marketing and testing new drugs is probably best illustrated by disasters and, after all, the problems of children reaching adolescence having been disabled all their lives are not to be ignored, despite on-going litigation. The question which is sometimes raised in relation to civil cases such as this one is whether or not it is right artificially to remove the possibility of the news media as well as anyone else giving advice to litigants. Giving advice to litigants is not at all an unacceptable practice and it is part of the duties of solicitors and barristers to advise their clients about whether to go to court, settle out of court, and even whether the monetary gains that might be achieved through court action are more than outweighed by the embarrassment, undesirable publicity, and time involved in the action. if there is nothing intrinsically wrong with such advice, how then can it be undesirable for the news media to offer similar advice?

Research Evidence on Prejudice

The above have been some of the arguments about the difficulties of pre-trial publicity and the related theme of contempt of court. It is clear that many of the issues are largely legal ones rather than psychological ones, but it is apparent also that psychological research may be relevant to part of the debate. The key reason why this is so is that the notion of prejudice requires that the chances of a fair trial are altered. We might be tempted to think of prejudicial publicity as that which will materially alter the verdict of the court. Of course, there can be no objective definition which can apply to a single case but as we shall see an objective definition is more possible in psychological research. Before I review the literature, I should point out that all the empirical evidence comes from the area of criminal law not civil law.

It is notable that the Committee on Contempt of Court (1975) produced no evidence of a social scientific nature on the effects of pre-trial publicity although there was a certain amount of evidence available then. They did present some slight evidence from the sort of natural experiments that I described earlier where as a consequence of being convicted at a slightly earlier trial, the accused had received full (in the case of the Kray's) and possibly prejudical publicity, just before a second trial. According to the Committee's report:

This is precisely the sort of material publication of which is normally prohibited by the law of contempt because of its potentially prejudicial effect. In the second trial the charge was again murder, but after being warned by the presiding judge not to be influenced by the publications the jury acquitted the defendants. Similarly, the jury who recently acquitted Miss Janie Jones of blackmail charges at the Old Bailey must have been well aware that she was convicted on other charges in a previous and highly publicised trial. (p. 23)

Whatever this proves, and it may well suggest that juries are far more wise than the law on contempt allows, perhaps we would like rather more formal evidence than this.

Most of the research evidence related to this issue is American and, for what it is worth, it is useful to note that the American data (Eimermann and Simon, 1970) suggests that as few as 1 per cent of criminal cases receive a line of publicity in the nation press and, in any case, the percentage of individuals pleading guilty is very high indeed, at somewhere between 75 per cent and 90 per cent of those processed through the courts. However, this does not mean that every case has a 1 per cent chance of being reported since coverage is selective and certain sorts of crimes are over-reported. We might expect these to be the more sensational, brutal and unusual crimes which may not be representative but do tend to attract readers. In local communities, served by more parochial newspapers, a greater proportion of individuals receive publicity in the local press (the figure is as high as 17 per cent) but it is two-and-a-half-times more likely that a crime brought before a jury will be reported.

Social scientists, in one notable case (Simon and Eimermann, 1971) gathered evidence which, as well as being relevant to our discussion, was used by the defence in an attempt to shift the location of the trial. Two men had been accused of the murder of a prominent local personality. Naturally, the crime attracted the attentions of the local press and received a lot of publicity though little, if any, of this publicity seemed prejudicial in the legal sense. However, the publicity left little doubt that the accused were vagrants and that there were witnesses to the events. There was no real evidence that the press was particularly irresponsible on this occasion but in this case there was a chance that the publicity would have a definite adverse effect on the accused. The researchers conducted a telephone survey of potential jurors a week before the trial. Of the potential jurors who agreed to co-operate, something like four-fifths had heard or read about the case and about three-fifths could provide some details about the crime. Sixty-five per cent of those who could remember details about the offence were in favour of the prosecution's case against the men, 27 per cent were indifferent, and the rest were unable to give any answers at all. Not one of them favoured the defence. That is, of all those who had been exposed to pre-trial publicity in this case, none of them thought that the defendants were innocent. In marked contrast to this, among those who were not able to supply details of the case, 41 per cent favoured the prosecution, 6 per cent favoured the defence, and 53 per cent were indifferent; that is, if you know nothing of the case, the overwhelming orientation is one of indifference about the guilt or innocence of the accused parties. Furthermore, it appears that this awareness made an impression on the evaluation of whether the defendants would receive a fair trial. More of those unable to supply details of the case than those able to provide such details thought that the defendant could expect a fair trial in that community. Although this was presented in court as evidence that juries from that community would be biased, it was rejected by the court. However, in what appears to be a remarkably equitable outcome, one of the two men pleaded guilty to the murder and was convicted, while the other was freed by the verdict of the jury!

As with any correlation study, this can be readily criticized – primarily because it is not possible to know whether exposure to publicity is a correlate or a cause of the expectations of the guilt of the accused.

Experimental research has inevitably come from simulated juries in mock-jury trials. This is not the place to go into detail about the worth of such methods but without them many areas of knowledge would be beyond investigation. In one experiment using mock juries, Kline and Jess (1966) divided the trials into two groups. In one half of the trials, the jurors received a copy of a newspaper containing a prejudicial account of the events leading up to the trial. In the other half of trials, the jurors received non-prejudicial versions of these same events. Of course, the newspapers used were identical in all other aspects. The study took place in a school of law and used real judges to direct the trial. After the evidence had been presented, the experimental and control juries all deliberated independently. No differences between the verdicts of the prejudiced and non-prejudiced juries were found. However, during their discussions, those juries which had been given the prejudiced information brought up this information, most of them rejecting it completely as a source of evidence. This rejection was largely on the basis of the judge's instructions concerning the proper sorts of evidence for the jury to consider in reaching their verdict. Those juries who did not reject entirely such evidence did not differ from the control juries in their verdicts.

Another piece of research (Simon, 1966) also used mock-jury trials but this time presented a sensational version of a pre-trial publicity sequence of news stories as the popular press might present it, or a version that might appear in a conservative newspaper, such as the *New York Times*. Before the trial, the respondents who had been presented with these different versions were asked to comment on the guilt or innocence of the accused. Then the subjects were exposed to a recording of an abbreviated trial consisting of an admonition from the judge, opening statements, testimony from witnesses and closing instructions from the judge. Finally, the jurors were once more asked to evaluate the guilt or innocence of the accused. The evidence clearly showed that pre-trial publicity seemed to have an effect on the pre-trial opinion of the jurors. First of all, they were willing to make judgements about the guilt of the accused, which presumably might not have been the case if it was not for the newspaper publicity. Secondly, for the sensational version of the stories, those jurors who read that the accused had a previous criminal record were less likely to believe him to be innocent. Furthermore, those who read the conservative version were more inclined to say that they had no opinion as to the guilt or innocence of the accused. However, after the hearing things changed. The trial had a big effect on the percentage feeling that the accused was not guilty. Whereas before the trial most seemed to think that the accused was guilty, after the trial the overwhelming majority considered him to be innocent.

If one were to go merely on the basis of this evidence I think that the following would be clear:

1 Pre-trial publicity is effective in creating judgements of guilt in the minds of the reader (see also Tans and Chaffee, 1966). Perhaps this is not surprising since the mere fact of arrest and going to court gives a big probability of guilt in the sense that most people eventually plead guilty. In this sense, pre-trial publicity is prejudicial.

2 Jurors seem capable of rejecting or making allowance for the effects of pre-trial publicity. In this sense, pre-trial publicity is not prejudicial (though whether or not some jurors will over- or under-compensate is a moot point).

But I must draw your attention to one study which seems on the surface of things to be rather in contradiction to the studies that I have so far described. This contradiction may appear more substantial than it actually is. Sue, Smith and Gilbert (1974) and Sue and Smith (1974) conducted an experiment which depended on ratings and not mock juries. The subjects read a transcript of a fictitious case which included a newspaper account of a description of the finding of the murder weapon in the accused's home which could not be presented in court because it was obtained by improper search procedures. In the other condition a gun was found which had no bearing on the case at all. In the transcript of the trial the judge either told the jury to disregard any pre-trial publicity or said nothing about it at all. The judge's instructions made little or no difference but the pre-trial publicity did have an effect – where the inadmissible but relevant evidence about the gun was given, the guilty verdicts were significantly more frequent than in the case where the weapon was irrelevant. It seems that the potential jurors were making allowance for the incriminating weapon even though this evidence could not be presented in court. Perhaps this is not surprising given that a legal technicality prevented the publication of these results. It might be worthwhile noting that the results of this study, as well as a similar one which presented evidence in court which was described as inadmissible or admissible in different experimental conditions, have greater implications for court room procedure than for the mass media since they imply that a fair trial cannot be achieved once inadmissible evidence has been presented. Personally it seems to me that this study on inadmissible evidence is the weakest, coming as it does from the least naturalistic of the research designs, and perhaps the most problematic of all areas of evidence.

Conclusions

In this short final section I would like to discuss some of the implications of the evidence and ideas brought forward so far. John Whale (1977) makes the following points in his book *The Politics of the Media*:

... the legal climate in which journalists work is a constantly changing one. The chief inhibitor of press freedom in the United Kingdom is the law. But the law is not carved on tablets of stone. It varies with the changes made in it by Parliament, the successive interpretations of it put forward by judges, and the use made of it by litigants (including Government); and all those variations are a distant expression of public opinion. At any time, therefore, journalists are in a state of some uncertainty about what the law is, and different editors treat it with different degrees of robustness. In the mid-1970s that uncertainty was increased by the existence of four weighty reports to the Government about aspects of press law, and the Government's slowness in deciding what to do about them. (p. 143)

The four reports Whale mentions are Phillimore on contempt, Younger on privacy, Faulks on defamation and Franks on secrecy. This amount of interest in the press is nothing new and controls on the press have historically been extensive and to some extent damaging. The reasons for wishing to control the news media are singular and simple: to prevent the news media controlling the public. Despite the rather dampened interpretations of the effects of the mass media which has developed out of more than half a century of mass media research, the fear of the power of publicity remains. It is no good the mass communications researcher suggesting that the press is relatively ineffective at creating and changing public opinion since the press may just once in a while be very effective in creating change.

The issue of the relationship between the news media and the law rarely becomes important as a matter of routine. It is only when the assumed freedom of the press and freedom of the courts are incompatible that major problems arise. Both of these freedoms, at best, are relative and in some ways it is very difficult to argue that one freedom is more important than the other. One can imagine circumstances in which the freedom of the press to make comment would be defensible particularly, perhaps, if the judiciary were adopting a highly political role. On the other hand, one can easily imagine an endless, scurrilous stream of publicity which would tip the balance of our judgement back away from the news media.

But all of this is to make the assumption that the news media are effective in prejudicing 'justice'. The data I have presented by and large do nothing to support this point of view. We could perhaps consider whether contempt should apply to the contents of the news media. Others have argued that it should only apply to trials before juries (given that we have other laws such as libel to cope with most unfair reporting) whereas the evidence that I have presented implies that for the most part juries are well able to disregard pre-trial publicity. In other words, their ability to judge is in this respect much the same as that assumed of the judiciary. Since an appeal presumably would not be heard before a jury, we might have a safety net should we ask to abolish contempt by publicity.

On the other hand, one suspects that there may well be little to be gained as a matter of routine by freeing the news media in this way. The news media have a mixed track record in relation to the courts. The present laws on contempt may well inhibit investigative journalism but so too does the economic climate. Freeing the press may make a marginal change but probably not a very big one. It is notable that the committee on contempt sat not as a consequence of endless brushes between the news media with endless issues to raise in relation to the public interest, but because the odd, extreme case, like the Thalidomide litigation raised issues out of the routine.

By all means, if we are to have a law on contempt that applies to the news media it should be clear, its limits well defined, and possible defences clarified, but do not let us make assumptions of a social scientific nature such as those of the power of the press and the malleability of the jury which are not supported by the evidence.

References

Chibnall, S. (1977), *Law-and-Order News*, London: Tavistock.

Committee on Contempt of Court (1975) *Report*, Cmnd 5794, London: HMSO.

Eimermann, T. and Simon, R. J. (1970), 'Newspaper coverage of crimes and trials: another empirical look at the free press–free trial controversy', *Journalism Quarterly*, **47** (1), 142–144.

Hain, P. (1976), *Mistaken Identity*, Quartet, London.

Howitt, D. and Cumberbatch, G. (1975), *Mass Media Violence and Society*, Elek, London.

Kline, F. G. and Jess, P. H. (1966), 'Prejudicial publicity: its effects on law school mock juries', *Journalism Quarterly*, **43** (1), 113–116.

Simon, R. J. (1966), 'Murder, juries and the press: does sensational reporting lead to verdicts of guilty?', *Transaction*, **3**, 40–42.

Simon, R. J. and Eimermann, T. (1971), 'The jury finds not guilty: another look at media influence on the jury', *Journalism Quarterly*, **48** (2), 343–344.

Sue, S. Smith, R. E. (1974), 'How not to get a fair trial,' *Psychology Today*, **7**, (12) 86–90.

Sue, S., Smith, R. E. and Gilbert, R. (1974), 'Biasing effects of pretrial publicity of judicial decisions', *Journal of Criminal Justice*, **2**, 163–171.

Tans, M. D. and Chaffee, S. H. (1966), 'Pretrial publicity and juror prejudice', *Journalism Quarterly*, **43**, 647–654.

Whale, J. (1977), *The Politics of the Media*, Fontana, London.

People, Probabilities and the Law

A. T. CARR *

The research upon which this paper is based is a spin-off from a series of experiments in which I have been investigating cognitive processes in anxiety. Some of the findings appear to have implications for the operation of legal processes. My intention is to focus upon an aspect of personality which has particular relevance to the activities of people who are concerned with the law, whether they are defendants, witnesses, jurors, magistrates or judges. This aspect of personality is of particular relevance to the law because it is involved in activities which can be described as probabilistic, for example decision-making, judgements of certainty and estimates of risk: and clearly, such activities are central to the application of the law. The aspect of personality concerned is the apparent consistency of individuals in their anticipations of events or outcomes with high positive or negative values. More specifically, it is the subjective likelihood which a person attaches to uncertain events, where these events or outcomes are very costly or very beneficial to the person.

It will be useful at this stage to clarify the meaning of the term 'subjective likelihood.' Just as one's personal or individual awareness of probabilities usually differs from objective or statistical probability, so subjective likelihood may differ from personal probability: it is an experience or feeling of likelihood as distinct from the deliberate or rational appraisal of probability one might make in a particular situation. Under certain circumstances one can be dramatically and painfully aware of this difference. In certain pathological states, for example obsessional disorders, this disparity is frequently expressed by a statement such as 'I *know* I won't get contaminated; you don't get contaminated after touching a door handle, my husband doesn't get contaminated after touching a door handle, nobody I know gets contaminated after touching door handles; yet I feel that I am *bound* to be contaminated if I do touch a door handle.' In such statements the individual is recognizing the difference between his deliberate and rational assessment of the likelihood of an outcome and his subjective experience of the likelihood of that outcome, his

---

*Department of Psychology, University of Leicester.

feeling of likelihood.

Such divergences between rational probability assessments and subjective likelihood are by no means confined to pathological states. Rather, they are readily observed in most of us under conditions where the relevant outcome has a high positive or negative value. Before illustrating this with some research results perhaps the concept of subjective likelihood can be clarified further by means of an hypothetical example. Imagine that you are on your way to a conference and, while sitting in the train, you take out of your case two identical brown manilla folders. In one of these is the final draft of an important paper you are preparing for publication and with it is the attached carbon, which is the only copy. In the other file are the details of the conference such as the programme and list of participants. When you arrive at your destination you discover that you have left both folders on the train. You hastily telephone the station and ask whether any files have been handed in. You are informed that one file has been handed in and you are asked to wait while the speaker goes to fetch this file. As you wait for him to return, how likely do you feel it is that the file he will bring is the one containing the only copy of the paper you are preparing for publication?

If we assume, reasonably, that the folders do not differ in relative value to any person who might have found them, then clearly the rational probability of the important folder being handed in is 50 per cent or thereabouts. However, on the basis of our results so far one would expect roughly six people in ten to feel that it was rather *unlikely* that the recovered folder was the one containing the paper and roughly three in ten to feel that it was *more than likely* that this folder had been handed in. Only about one in ten would feel that it was no more or less likely that the recovered folder was the one containing the paper rather than the one containing details of the conference. The point being made is that the costs and benefits of outcomes influence our expectations: they displace subjective likelihood away from rational probability. This effect is an individual difference occurring to different degrees and in different directions for different people. However, for any one individual the effect appears to be consistent across outcomes having the same sign (in other words, across outcomes which are highly favourable, and across outcomes which are highly unfavourable) independent of the details of the outcomes.

At this point I can briefly discuss those aspects of my work on anxiety which have incidentally provided some information of apparent relevance to legal processes. In this work, I have used a number of procedures involving a sequence of events leading, eventually, to a possible electric shock. The subjects have experience of the shock prior to an experimental run and the shock level is set at the same subjective level of painfulness for each subject. At various points in the sequence which leads to an outcome of shock or no shock, the subject is required to indicate on a sliding scale how likely he feels it is that a certain event, which contributes to the final outcome, will occur. The discussion which follows will be confined to one of the earliest and simplest procedures in order to illustrate the approach and types of results obtained.

Fifty black and 50 white beads were mixed together in a cloth bag in front of the subject. Fifty-one draws were to be made from this bag by the experimenter and the subject was to keep a tally of the number of black and white beads drawn. After each draw the drawn bead was replaced in the bag. The subject was told that he would receive the predetermined level of electric shock if 26 or more black beads were drawn overall: the shock would be delivered automatically upon the drawing of the 26th black bead. Prior to each draw the subject indicated on a sliding scale how likely he felt it was that a black bead would be drawn on that particular trial. The scale was a 10 cm line marked at one end with 'not at all likely, virtually impossible' and at the other with 'extremely likely, virtually definite'. The scale was not marked in any other way and the subject moved a slider to indicate his feeling of likelihood, this slider being returned to alternate extremes of the scale between draws. Using a specially constructed bag it was arranged that on draw 50 a total of 25 white and 25 black beads should have been accumulated although, of course, the arrival at these totals had been appropriately staggered in a random and identical fashion for each subject.

It soon became clear that there were at least two distinct patterns of response in terms of subjective likelihoods. Of the 48 subjects who completed this study, 28 gave subjective likelihoods on the 51st trial which were significantly higher than 50 per cent and 15 reported subjective likelihoods which were significantly lower than 50 per cent. Out of interest I decided to look separately at these two groups, defined by their response on the last draw as *negative maximizers* and *negative minimizers* respectively. Within each of these groups the mean of the subjective likelihoods reported by the subjects was computed for every fifth draw. The groups were arbitrarily defined as consisting of those subjects whose subjective likelihoods on draw 51 were more than 5 per cent above 50 per cent and those whose subjective likelihoods were more than 5 per cent below 50 per cent. Those subjects whose final responses fell between these limits were treated as a third group. The different patterns of responses over the 51 trials can be seen in Figure 1.

It is quite clear from these data that not only are there two obviously divergent trends but that there is a third, much smaller group, whose subjective likelihoods deviate not at all from a rational appraisal of probability. Intuitively, and in view of Epstein's work (1972) with count-down procedures

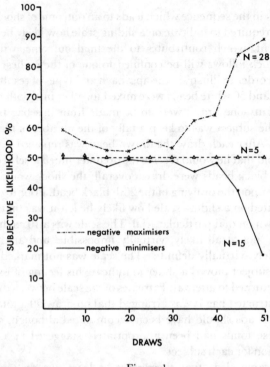

Figure 1

using objective probabilities, it is not at all surprising to note that the members of the negative maximizing group were significantly more anxious (on self-report and autonomic measures) than were the members of the negative minimizing group.

A short series of studies was then run to see whether the individual differences observed in this first experiment were consistent across different outcomes and different procedures. The first procedure was used again with a positive outcome (food after 14 hours starvation). Detailed situation descriptions were used with highly positive or highly negative outcomes (waiting for the results of an interview for a much desired job or returning to the doctor for the results of tests, respectively). Also, a self-administered questionnaire of 20 items was used: this depicted situations with highly positive or highly negative outcomes. As in the count-down studies, subjects were required to indicate how likely they felt it was that the outcome in question would transpire.

Interestingly, the original separation into negative maximizers and mini-mizers held up well provided that the signs of the outcomes in question remained negative, in that the distributions of subjective likelihoods for the two groups overlapped very little. However, membership of the negative maximizing or minimizing group was no predictor of response in relation to outcomes with a high *positive* value. In other words, being a negative maximizer, for example, gives no indication of the person's tendency to maximize or minimize the subjective likelihood of positive outcomes. Nevertheless, there was some consistency for individuals within positive outcomes, although this was less than that observed within negative outcomes, with a greater degree of overlap between the distributions of subjective likelihoods for the positive maximizers and minimizers. One of the reasons for the lower consistency might be that positive outcomes were not rated by subjects as highly positive as they had negatively rated the negative outcomes. Figure 2 shows the numbers of subjects who were consistent in maximizing or minimizing the likelihood of negative outcomes and in maximizing or minimizing the likelihood of positive outcomes. The numbers in the cells of the figure show the numbers of subjects who consistently exhibited each of the possible combinations of maximizing and minimizing the likelihoods of positive and negative outcomes.

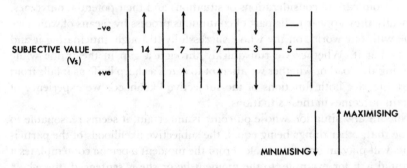

Figure 2

The principal results shown in the figure indicate that two thirds of the subjects showed clear consistency within both positive and negative outcomes and across different procedures and different outcomes. This suggests strongly that an individual's style of maximizing and minimizing the subjective likelihood of outcomes constitutes a stable aspect of his temperament or personality.

Of course, an interaction between subjective value and subjective probability has long been suspected. In the early 1960s Edwards (1962) rued this possibility because of the implications for utility theory. Also, there are other data which reveal individual differences in the interaction of value and subjective likelihood (Slovic, 1966). However, the striking result here is the consistency of such interaction effects for individuals using different procedures and different outcomes, particularly when the outcomes concerned have a high negative value. In a review of this field in 1971, Lee concluded that 'subjective probabilities appear to interact with the values of the associated consequences', but he had very little data upon which to base this statement. It would appear that serendipity has brought us a little closer to a position of validating his tentative conclusion.

Space precludes a more detailed presentation of data and further discussion of the more general issues. However, let us recapitulate before proceeding with the specific argument concerning the operation of legal processes. First, the subjective likelihood of an event is, for most people, a function of the subjective value of the event. Second, this interaction effect appears to be an individual difference in that it is consistent across situations for any one person, at least for highly negative outcomes. Third, under certain specific conditions subjective likelihood may be a significant variable, exerting a sizeable effect upon the outcome. In the shock-anticipation study for example, those who saw the shock as most likely were significantly more anxious.

It is worth stressing at this point that although subjective likelihoods may result from careful considerations of situations and their potential outcomes, typically they appear to be part of continuous process by means of which we cope with our world, on the whole successfully, through anticipating it and predicting it. Whether we run quickly through a gap in the traffic while crossing the road or whether we attempt to catch a sharp knife as it falls from the table, are both functions of the subjective likelihoods we experience of certain outcomes in these situations.

Now in any situation whose outcome is uncertain, it seems reasonable to argue that, other things being equal, the subjective likelihoods of the participants will play an important role. From the moment a person contemplates a criminal act, for example, to the moment he or she is sentenced, the whole process is a succession of uncertain events in which the behaviours and emotions of the people involved will be influenced by their individual styles of maximizing or minimizing the subjective likelihoods of positive and negative outcomes. The act of taking and driving away a motor vehicle or that of making a probation order are both probabilistic, involving either deliberate or intuitive and relatively immediate assessments of the costs and benefits of certain outcomes and their likelihoods. It follows therefore that if there are large and consistent individual differences in the tendency of people to maximize or minimize the likelihoods of certain outcomes, as these results and other data indicate, then the degrees of certainty expressed by witnesses, the deliberations of jurors and the actions of judges may be as much a function of individual style as of careful considerations of the 'facts' of a case.

By way of illustration consider a youth who, while aimlessly wandering the suburban night streets, encounters a woman walking towards him down a poorly lit road. For whatever reason, and not unusually, the neutral (that is, without intention) thought crosses his mind that it would be quite simple to snatch her handbag and make off with it. Being a negative minimizer and also possibly a positive maximizer, he is not aware of any real possibility that he could be unsuccessful, observed, identified, or apprehended. Perhaps because he is bored, angry or frustrated by lack of cash, the idea becomes an intention, the intention a plan and the mugging takes place. In the process the woman is knocked to the ground and suffers head injury.

Contrary to his expectation the youth is later picked up by the police on the report of an eye-witness and he is subsequently included in an identification parade. The task for the eye-witness is not any easy one; the street was poorly lit, and since he is an empathic person and also a negative maximizer, the subjective likelihood of his incorrectly identifying somebody is particularly high. Consequently, the eye-witness is unable positively to identify the subject. In the absence of a positive identification the case against the youth is not very strong. Nevertheless the police officer concerned, being a positive maximizer, feels that it is worth prosecuting the case in the light of the rather weak evidence that does exist.

In court the demeanour of the police officer giving evidence is one of confidence: being a positive maximizer he has the strong expectation that the case will be successful. Similarly, the demeanour of the defendant is one of confidence and relaxation since, being a negative minimizer, he does not feel that he is likely to be convicted. Also, because he is not anxious he will not be slow in making decisions; he will be able to answer quickly and readily, and will be more able to provide plausible explanations concerning his where-abouts and activities. The demeanour of the eye-witness in court is one of uncertainty and caution, his being a negative maximizer, and the result is largely unconvincing testimony. The parents of the youth, being negative maximizers and feeling that the crime of which their son is accused is a dreadful thing, feel that the likelihood of his being convicted is very high. Consequently, they behave in ways which are consonant with their believing that he had actually committed the crime. Indeed, in the absence of an overriding belief in the virtues of their son, being negative maximizers they may well feel that the chances of his actually having committed the crime are quite high. Either way, their behaviour indicates an expectation that their son will be convicted. Also, in their anxiety, which is not due to their having to appear in court, and which is not therefore amenable to reduction by careful handling by Counsel, they are not able to provide alternative and plausible explanations for his absence from home that evening. The alternatives they do proffer are stated hesitatingly and without conviction. The result favours the prosecution a good deal more than the defence.

The judge, being one of those rare individuals for whom subjective likelihood is unaffected by subjective value, gives a well balanced summing-up and the jury retire. The most influential of the jurors is empathically concerned for the highly negative effects of a conviction for this family and the youth, and being a negative maximizer, speaks strongly and eloquently for the youth's innocence, emphasizing the lack of firm evidence for his guilt. When the jury return the youth is acquitted: he is not surprised for this was the outcome he expected. The parents are surprised but relieved for they expected their son to be convicted. The police officer is surprised and feels that justice has not been done. The eye-witness, being a negative maximizer, is sure that the decision is wrong and feels that he should have spoken up more positively. Finally, and rather more seriously, the victim recovers from her injuries but, being a negative maximizer, she becomes agoraphobic.

The speculative nature of this hypothetical example is clear. The intention is only to illustrate the many points at which subjective likelihoods can exercise an influence upon the proceedings rather than to argue for their critical importance as determiners of the outcome. Obviously there is a vast amount of research work to be done, particularly on the expectations of offenders. Currently I am planning to look at subjective likelihoods in a group of young offenders which, it is hoped, will throw some light upon the factors influencing impulsive crime.

As a final note it is worth mentioning that since the utility of a behaviour or strategy is a function of both subjective likelihood and subjective value, the use of severe sentencing to achieve a deterrent effect might have the desired effect for negative maximizers, but might have just the opposite effect for negative minimizers. For this latter group the relevant strategy, in terms of preventing crime, would seem to be to raise the objective probability of being convicted and rely upon the positive relationship between subjective and objective probability to achieve the effect. Clearly, this raises the issue of the models used by judges when considering sentence, whether rehabilitative, punitive/reparative, deterrent, etc. If rehabilitative models are being used, then detailed knowledge of the defendant would be crucial, in determining an appropriate sentence and perhaps this is one of the stages at which the expertise of psychologists could be used.

References

Edwards, W. (1962), 'Subjective probabilities inferred from decisions', *Psychological Review*, **69**, 109–135.

Epstein, S. (1972), 'The nature of anxiety with emphasis upon its relationship for expectancy', In Spielberger, C. D. (ed.), *Anxiety: Current Trends in Theory and Research*, Academic Press, London. pp. 291–337.

Lee, W. (1971), *Decision Theory and Human Behaviour*, John Wiley, Chichester.

Slovic, P. (1966), 'Value as a determiner of subjective probability', *IEEE Transactions on Human Factors in Electronics*, **7**, 22–28.